How to Kick Your Writer's Block To The Curb

By Christina Hamlett

DEDICATION

To one of my dearest and most prolific writer friends,
Peter S. Fischer (*Columbo, Murder, She Wrote, Ellery
Queen* and squillions of other television shows
I couldn't get enough of.)
Even after he left Hollywood, his fertile imagination
had no intention of retiring. Every time he writes a
new book for The Hollywood Murder Mystery Series
(and there have been many so far!), yours truly is
honored to give each manuscript its first read
and to tell him what I think.
Peter also gifted me with something that is as
treasured as his friendship—
his 50+ year old manual typewriter
on which he typed all of the original *Columbo* and
Murder, She Wrote scripts.
I only hope with the passage of time
that I will do it justice.

TABLE OF CONTENTS

"All writing problems are psychological problems. Blocks usually stem from the fear of being judged. If you imagine the world listening, you'll never write a line. That's why privacy is so important. You should write first drafts as if they will never be shown to anyone."
— **Erica Jong**

"Who is more to be pitied, a writer bound and gagged by policemen or one living in perfect freedom who has nothing more to say?"
— **Kurt Vonnegut Jr.**

"Biting my truant pen, beating myself for spite: 'Fool!' said my muse to me, 'look in thy heart, and write.'"
— **Philip Sidney**

"The music lets me see the story but the story doesn't let me write the words."
— **Elizabeth J. Kolodziej**

"Don't waste time waiting for inspiration. Begin, and inspiration will find you."
— **H. Jackson Brown Jr.**

"Very often we write down a sentence *too early*, then another *too late;* what we have to do is write it down at the proper time, otherwise it's lost."
— **Thomas Bernhard**

Writer's Block:

When your imaginary
friends stop talking
to you.

INTRODUCTION

You fail only if you stop writing.
-Ray Bradbury

Whether or not you have ever aspired to be a published author, the mental paralysis known as writer's block can likely trace its origins to elementary school.

The first day back from summer vacation, how many of you had teachers who gave the not-so-original assignment to write an essay about how you spent your time during that three-month break? Although you remembered every detail and may have even talked about it incessantly with all your friends, the problem was channeling those memories into something that would actually look good on paper and get you an A.

Compounding the problem was the angst that your summer experience—even if it *was* well written—might not stack up in the coolness equation against your classmates. *They* went on a family vacation to Machu Picchu. *They* learned how to play Lacrosse. *They* started a community garden for a homeless shelter.

You watched movies, walked the dog and collected Pokémon cards.

When you stood up to read your essay, were you nervous it would be to the deafening sound of crickets?

How can you even motivate yourself to get started when you're already dreading how the finished product will be received? The fear of the blank page—or the blank computer screen—looms larger with each tick of the clock and it doesn't get any easier into adulthood.

Maybe it wouldn't be so bad if you could just come up with the perfect first sentence.

Except that there isn't one. Further, the longer you keep waiting for the perfect first sentence to materialize, the longer it will take to ever write the *second* sentence. And the third. And so forth.

Writer's block is defined as being (1) unable to think of what to write, and (2) unable to think of how to proceed if you *do* have something to write. Inherent in both of these conditions is the twofold issue of commitment and consequence.

Some people work better under the pressure of deadlines that have been imposed by others. If, for instance, they have two weeks to prepare a written report for their boss, they'll be burning the midnight oil on Sunday because they know they can't show up empty-handed on Monday morning. Their next job appraisal, in fact, may depend on how well they manage time-sensitive assignments.

Others freak out and suffer from performance anxiety that, no matter *what* they do, it won't be their best effort. Unlike the person who does absolutely nothing for two weeks and then races to the finish line, there are those who will spend every waking moment of those same two weeks stressing about each word and each sentence and making it more agonizing than a root canal. Sound familiar?

When the stakes are high and the timeline for completion has been set by an external force—a boss, a teacher, a publisher—it's critical to commit to the task or suffer a real (or perceived) consequence. While in most cases the worst that can happen is simply being asked to do it over and fix any problem verbiage and/or structure, one's sense of worry can be blown out of proportion if it courts any possible stigma of personal rejection.

But what about the scenario of an individual who has always talked about writing a novel or a screenplay someday … and yet has a boatload of excuses as to why s/he hasn't started it? The difference is that if there's no outside pressure, no deadline and no expectation of a deliverable, there's also no risk, no incentive to move a project forward, and no danger of being excluded or ostracized. Even if the first tentative steps *have* been taken to get an idea out of one's head and into printed words, writer's block is still likely to manifest in the following ways:

- ✔ Self-doubt. *"It seemed like such a blockbuster idea when I began but now it just feels stupid."*
- ✔ Boredom. *"I'm getting tired of my characters. I wish they could just finish this book by themselves."*
- ✔ Mental Cul de Sac. *"I've led my plot into a dead end and have no idea how to get out of it."*
- ✔ Distractions. *"Oooooh, cat videos! I think I'll watch these for a while so I don't have to work on my novel."*
- ✔ Rewrite Ad Nauseum. *"Maybe I should just go back to the beginning and rewrite the whole thing."*

While the goal of this book is to supply you with enough creative ideas and story-starters that writer's block will never darken your door, there's a correlation between writing and exercising that I'd like you to remember. Specifically, you can buy a membership to the best gym in your neighborhood and have access to the most state-of-the-art equipment for working out, but if you never go, what good is all of it doing you?

In a nutshell, no one's going to come to your house to ask you why you're not at the gym. Unless you have a personal coach or a work-out buddy to keep you accountable and focused, an exercise regimen can be just as solitary a pursuit as trying to become a more accomplished writer. I'm reminded of a colleague's stay-at-home mum who had bulging shelves of how-to books about writing, a nice computer and printer, and the same 24 hours a day as anyone else on the planet. And yet in the 30+ years I knew her, she never wrote a thing.

The first step to kicking your new regimen into gear is to ask someone you trust to become your wordsmithing trainer. This individual need not be a fellow writer but s/he *does* need to stay on task in asking you every few days how your writing is going. Even better, s/he needs to be able to *read* what you've written so you'll know you can't fake your progress. *("But of <u>course</u> I did 300 push-ups and ran 10 miles yesterday when no one was watching…")*

Initially, this well-meaning dynamic may tempt you to channel your inner Gene Wilder from *Young Frankenstein* when he instructs Igor and Inga:

> *"No matter what you hear in there, no matter how cruelly I beg you, no matter how terribly I may scream, do not open this door or you will undo everything I have worked for. Do you understand? Do not open this door."*

This directive is then immediately followed by:

> *"Let me out. Let me out of here. Get me the hell out of here. What's the matter with you people? I was joking! Don't you know a joke when you hear one?"*

If your trainer is as serious about encouraging your career as *you* should be, s/he will not let you out of the room .. or off the hook.

I applied this wisdom to my own writing habits years ago when I told several of my coworkers I was going to write a romantic suspense novel. Turns out this was a genre they loved and so they asked if they could read my chapters in progress. I agreed to this but told them they needed to help me keep to a firm schedule of a new chapter every single week.

Since I knew I couldn't face them on Monday mornings without chapter copies in my hand—nor could I start a pattern of calling in sick—I was able to finish that first book in six months. A year and a half later—still following this regimen with my volunteer trainers—I had completed three more romantic suspense novels and subsequently sold all of them to HarperCollins.

If you don't as yet have a book or script project in mind, don't worry. You can easily use any of the warm-up exercises in this book to start building your brain muscles and developing smart habits. Simply show your trainer the exercise, decide on a deadline to complete it … and start writing. Whether you compose a few paragraphs or a few pages of flash fiction, save all of your efforts in a special file that you can revisit at a later time and perhaps develop further.

Keep in mind as well the psychological aspect of creating a daily "habit" of writing. Studies have shown that if you want to successfully incorporate a new routine into your life, you need to do it for 21 days straight. By Day 22, you can't *not* do it.

What this means, however, is that you can't *skip* any days during this trial period. No weekends off, no holidays, no promising yourself you'll make up for it. It's like cheating on a diet. Once you start sneaking cookies on the sly and telling yourself that you'll just eat celery for the rest of the week to counter the caloric damage—well, you get the picture.

If you write every single day for 9 days and then decide to goof off for a while, the 21-day-clock starts all over from the very beginning. Seriously. The same goes for taking a break after Day 19. So close, and yet so far …

Will everything you come up with during this period be brilliant? Probably not. Then again, could you expect to run your first marathon after only a couple of really sweaty hours on a treadmill? If the marathon is that important to you, you'll find a way to stay the course and incrementally build your strength. Likewise, if becoming a confident and accomplished writer is on your list of goals, you'll find the steadfastness to out-run the obstacles and excuses that have been holding you back and turn them into a tiny blip in the rearview mirror.

Christina Hamlett

CHAPTER 1
SNAPPY ONE-LINERS

In the introduction, I talked about the challenge of coming up with a catchy first line. But what if someone were to just *give* you a bunch of opening lines to take off and run with? That's what the exercises in this chapter are all about. You can use them as the jumping-off point for a short story, an article, a novel, a line of dialogue in a play, or just a few stream-of-consciousness paragraphs based on your personal interpretation of what the line means. The only rule is that you have to use the line exactly as written and it needs to be your opening sentence.

The Fortune Cookie

I love to use this exercise in workshops because all of my participants get a tasty snack while they're mulling what to do with the paper message inside. The next time you get Chinese food, save the cookie's contents for inspiration. Meanwhile, feel free to give these a trial run:

- ✓ *Hard work pays off in the future; laziness pays off now.*
- ✓ *Patience is bitter but its fruit is sweet.*
- ✓ *A beautiful, smart and loving person will be coming into your life.*
- ✓ *The simplest answer is to act.*
- ✓ *A bargain is something you don't need at a price you can't resist.*
- ✓ *An unexpected relationship will become permanent.*
- ✓ *Your mouth may be moving but no one is listening.*
- ✓ *Do not fear what you don't know.*

You can also open virtual fortune cookies online at:

http://www.myfortunecookie.co.uk/
http://www.fortunecookiemessage.com/
https://www.astrology.com/game/fortune-cookie.html
http://zippytech.com/cookie/fortunecookie.php.

Who Said It

This exercise gives you a multiplicity of pairings for an opening line of dialogue in any genre or setting. The first step is to choose a line from Column A, a word from Column B and a character from Column C. The second step is to write what that character says next.

For example:

"I'm quitting first chance I get," declared the tomb raider. "All these mummy curses are freaking me out."

"I know it's here somewhere," murmured the psychic. "How do you lose a crystal ball?"

"I'm not a miracle worker," said the realtor. "I can't make the closets any bigger."

A	B	C
"I don't have the money,"	said	the librarian.
"Why should I care?"	replied	the hairdresser.
"You said it wasn't a problem,"	asked	the teenager.
"Are we lost?"	whispered	the janitor.
"Someone's coming,"	insisted	the actor.
"Is this the face of a liar?"	retorted	the bookkeeper.
"I'm quitting first chance I get,"	murmured	the garbage collector.
"I should have known better,"	screamed	the thief.
"I think we should start over,"	declared	the lawyer.
"Not your best decision,"	stated	the politician.
"You don't know what it's like,"	promised	the postal worker.
"I only have eyes for you,"	announced	the tomb raider.
"I can't go out there,"	bragged	the night clerk.
"I'm not a miracle worker,"	lied	the doctor.
"I can have it here tomorrow,"	confessed	the realtor.
"I shouldn't have answered,"	chided	the bride.
"I know it's here somewhere,"	explained	the counselor.
"If I had a million dollars,"	shouted	the soldier.
"I just work here,"	warned	the doorman.
"What, exactly, do you want?"	argued	the conductor.
"You know I should have won,"	complained	the psychic.
"I really shouldn't do this,"	countered	the coach.
"I just want to go home,"	interrupted	the orphan.
"Nothing has worked so far,"	commented	the investigator.
"I don't believe any of it,"	quipped	the pilot.

Call Me Ishmael

We have no idea how long it took the authors of the following books to come up with their opening lines. We do know, however, that some of those first lines went on to become almost as famous as the novels themselves:

- It was the best of times, it was the worst of times.—Charles Dickens, *A Tale of Two Cities* (1859)
- It is a truth universally acknowledged, that a single man in possession of a good fortune, must be in want of a wife. —Jane Austen, *Pride and Prejudice* (1813)
- All children, except one, grow up. –J.M. Barrie, *Peter Pan* (1911)
- Call me Ishmael. —Herman Melville, *Moby-Dick* (1851)
- Happy families are all alike; every unhappy family is unhappy in its own way. —Leo Tolstoy, *Anna Karenina*
- Mrs. Dalloway said she would buy the flowers herself. —*Virginia Woolf*, Mrs. Dalloway (1925)
- It was a dark and stormy night.—Edward George Bulwer-Lytton, *Paul Clifford* (1830)
- I have never begun a novel with more misgiving. —W. Somerset Maugham, *The Razor's Edge* (1944)
- He was born with a gift of laughter and a sense that the world was mad. —Raphael Sabatini, *Scaramouche* (1921)
- There was no possibility of taking a walk that day. –Charlotte Brontë, *Jane Eyre* (1847)
- Mr. and Mrs. Dursley, of number four, Privet Drive, were proud to say that they were perfectly normal, thank you very much. –JK Rowling, *Harry Potter and the Sorcerer's Stone* (1998)

For this exercise, you are tasked with rewriting the opening line of whatever novel you are currently reading without altering the line's original intention. Examples:

"Taking a walk that day was totally unthinkable."

"Major unease underscores the story I'm about to start."

"It goes without saying that a wealthy bachelor needs to find a bride."

Closing Statements

It was Mickey Spillane who said, "The first chapter sells the book; the last chapter sells the next book." We're going to take this approach a step further and look at the final *sentence* in some popular literature:

- So we beat on, boats against the current, borne back ceaselessly into the past. –F. Scott Fitzgerald, *The Great Gatsby* (1925)
- He was soon borne away by the waves and lost in darkness and distance. –Mary Shelley, *Frankenstein* (1818)
- In your rocking-chair, by your window, shall you dream such happiness as you may never feel. –Theodore Dreiser, *Sister Carrie* (1900)
- She was seventy-five and she was going to make some changes in her life. –Jonathan Franzen, *The Corrections* (2001)
- In a place far away from anyone or anywhere, I drifted off for a moment. –Haruki Murakami, *The Wind-Up Bird Chronicle* (1994)
- It is a far, far better thing that I do, than I have ever done; it is a far, far better rest that I go to than I have ever known. –Charles Dickens, *A Tale of Two Cities* (1859)
- Are there any questions? –Margaret Atwood, *The Handmaid's Tale* (1986)
- The old man was dreaming about the lions. –Ernest Hemingway, *The Old Man and the Sea* (1952)
- After all, tomorrow is another day. –Margaret Mitchell, *Gone with the Wind* (1936)
- After a while I went out and left the hospital and walked back to the hotel in the rain. –Ernest Hemingway, *A Farewell to Arms* (1929)

For this exercise, you'll use one of the lines above as the *starting* sentence of a new novel. You'll then write a line that immediately follows it. Note: It doesn't have to be a sequel to the original, just whatever inspires and tweaks your imagination. Example:

"The old man was dreaming about the lions. Maybe he should see if the circus had any entry-level jobs he could apply for."

TV Teasers

Long before there were Internet spoilers and streaming trailers to clue us in about upcoming episodes of our favorite television shows, there was *TV Guide* and its one-line teasers:

Rhoda asks Mary for a loan.
A woman from Starsky's past reveals a secret.
Micaela's professional ethics are called into question.
Scarecrow has amnesia and thinks Amanda is his wife.
The Fonz gets selected for jury duty.
Jessica's nephew is arrested for murder.
Hoss is asked to judge a cutest baby contest.
Endora turns Darrin into a lamp.
The Professor discovers the island is sinking.
Angelique takes revenge on Quentin.

Rarely were/are these write-ups more than 10 words—just enough to grab viewers' imaginations and cause them to think, "I wonder how this problem turns out. Maybe I should watch."

Using this minimalist approach, your assignment is to take the most recent television series you have watched and write 10-words-or-less teasers for three episodes you best remember. Since you can assume the fan base already knows the characters' names, occupations, and the show's setting/premise, you don't have to spend any verbiage explaining these elements. Likewise, if there are multiple sub-plots in play during an episode, focus on the one which you believe constitutes the most substantive or intriguing hook.

This exercise is especially fun to do with soap operas, even though their themes tend to be a tad repetitive:

_____ catches _____ with _____.
_____ reveals the truth about _____'s baby.
_____ crashes _____ and _____'s wedding.
_____'s addiction forces a _____ with _____.
_____ and _____ conspire against _____.
_____ begs _____ for another chance.
A dying _____ tells _____ about _____.

#Twitterpated

The popularity of Twitter's 140-character limit derives from two things:

1. The standard length of SMS (short messaging service) text for cell phones is 160-characters, allowing users to send a "tweet" and still have room left to include their name.
2. Many people have the attention span of gnats. They want the gratification of getting an instant sound-bite without having to read several paragraphs. It also, of course, fuels the tweeters' need to have followers who are totally riveted by everything they post:

 @zoomygirl
Ate the best oatmeal ever for my breakfast this morning. May do it again tomorrow or on Saturday and add some raisins!

On the plus side, Twitter has encouraged people to write more economically (notwithstanding abbreviations and Internet slang acronyms) and use as few words as possible to get their point across. It even has application as a self-editing tool in the event you're asked to whittle down an article that exceeds a publisher's word-cap.

If you are already an ardent tweeter, this exercise will be an easy one for you. Write down six things you did today. Whether the things on your list are silly or profound, convert each of them to one-sentence tweets that don't exceed 140-characters.

Need an additional challenge? What are the top three headlines in today's newspaper? Turn each of them into tweets that will not only hook the attention of your Twitter tribe but will distill the articles' most crucial information to 140-characters or less.

Truth or Tabloid?

Bubbles the Chimp Marries Former Child Star!
DNA Proves Vlad the Impaler Was a Woman!
Lost Civilization Found Living at Center of Earth!
Termites Devour Man's Wooden Leg While He Sleeps!
Conjoined Twins Each Give Birth To Triplets!
Giant Asteroid To Hit Our Planet This Christmas!
Juggling Pig Runs in Boston Marathon ... and Wins!
Lemmings Overrun Village Rather Than Jumping Off Cliff!
King Tut's Mummy Plays Poker with Aliens in Parking Lot!
NASA Astrophysicists Confirm Our Moon Is Hollow!
Bigfoot Sighting After-Hours at Philadelphia Mall!
Chihuahua Drives Owner to Hospital Emergency Room!
Cloned Tyrannosaurus Rex Bites British Prime Minister!
Wood from Noah's Ark Found at Fargo Yard Sale!
Cosmetics Heiress Leaves Her Estate to Pet Hamster!
Half of World Leaders Are Extraterrestrials!
Housewife Finds Elvis Living in Her Basement!

You've just got to love the wackiness of supermarket tabloids, not to mention that they give you something to do while you're waiting in line to have your groceries rung up. I sometimes wonder if the staffers of these publications sit around tossing out the most insane scenarios ever just to see who can deliver the craziest idea.

For this exercise, it's *your* turn to create faux headlines in 10 words or less. And if you really feel inspired, take one of your headlines to the next level and create a fake "well researched" article with quotes to go with it.

Classified Intel

Classified ads date back to the time of Ancient Egypt where the locals used to carve hieroglyphics into outdoor public spaces so as to hawk items for sale. From there, it was a hop, skip and a jump across time to 17th century England and the emergence of printed handbills to announce town meetings, locate lost property and sometimes even to seek a mate.

By the time similar ads made it to America, it was in the context of newspaper fillers and primarily focused on land sales, legal disclaimers and transportation. Today, classifieds still fill a purpose of offloading goods, finding affordable housing, posting employment opportunities and, yes, seeking companionship.

To the amusement of the rest of us, proofreading is not always a priority for individuals writing their own copy.

- ✓ *For sale: Antique desk suitable for lady with thick legs and large drawers.*
- ✓ *Wanted: Man to take care of horse that does not smoke or drink.*
- ✓ *Experienced stripper wanted for home improvement project.*
- ✓ *Free dog to good home. Eats anything and is especially fond of small children.*
- ✓ *Wanted: Unmarried girls to pick fresh fruit and produce at night.*
- ✓ *Mature Schnauzer. Very good poet for small apartment.*
- ✓ *Need caregiver for grandmother who can lift 200 pounds and has lots of experience.*
- ✓ *Will trade one night stand for used baby stroller.*
- ✓ *Dependable chef wanted, must be willing to get hands dirty.*

Now it's *your* turn to get creative with a classified ad, the objective being to pen something wherein the spelling, punctuation placement and/or wrong word might convey an alternative meaning.

Example:

For sale: Early American monogamy and pine bedroom furniture for antique lovers.

CHAPTER 2
THE BLOG! THE BLOG!

According to Statistica (https://www.statistica.com), the cumulative total of Tumblr blogs from May 2011 to July 2017 surpassed 357.7 million … and that's not even counting all the *other* social media portals where participants are rabbiting on about anything, everything and nothing.

Maybe you're a serial blogger yourself and have attracted a following of readers interested in your views on politics, road-trips, movies, raising baby goats, today's dating scene or how to make the best pizza.

And yet writer's block has selectively stymied you from officially starting work on the book you've been saying you're going to write someday. Surprise! The book has *already* been started but you just haven't realized it yet because you were too busy … blogging.

A case in point is a colleague of mine who has been faithfully blogging for the last six years. Readers love her humorous essays about her looney family members and have been telling her she should write a book.

"But a book takes way too much time," she replies.

Can you see where I'm going with this?

At two blogs a week for six years, she now has over 600 essays—more than enough to start stitching her favorites together into the very book she says she doesn't have the time to start writing from scratch.

Not surprisingly, this is the way a lot of bloggers *do* make the transition to a different platform, especially if their content is nonfiction; i.e., how-to articles, anecdotal/humorous/memoir, inspirational, culinary.

Even better is the fact that they have an existing fan base on their blog site and can share information about the book's progress, publishing date, book-signings, etc. Couple this with the angst that writers often feel re: Will people like what I have to say? Well, those people are already your online peeps and will probably feel quite chuffed at having been the ones to encourage you.

If Inspector Javert Blogged

Mon Dieu! My eyes cannot have deceived me, not yet again. It is a face I would know anywhere, though these past years he has changed his name as easily as he changes clothes. I was crossing Boulevard de Rochechouart when I happened to glance in the direction of a small boulangerie. There, in the dim light of the alley, a profile most familiar. What was that small parcel clutched so closely to his breast, a parcel he obviously sought to hide? A loaf of bread, perhaps? But, of course! It was a stolen loaf that first set my nemesis, Jean Valjean, on his path of criminal intent. Clearly he has not deviated from his wicked quest to procure baked goods without appropriate payment. I shall make the proper notation in my journal and return on the morrow to see if he reappears, ignorant of my dogged presence in the shadows.

Your assignment: Choose any famous fictional character from a book published prior to 1920. Examples: Captain Ahab, Count Dracula, Jane Eyre, Roxanne, Maid Marian. Compose a first-person humorous blog between 300 and 500 words. The blog can either be a single-day entry or reflect multiple days as long as the 500-word cap is not exceeded.

This blog exercise need not emulate the literary style of the source material (i.e., Shakespeare) but it's certainly welcome if you do it particularly well. The stronger emphasis is on humor that captures the dreams, fears, neuroses and egos of the characters chosen.

Lastly, the blog must focus on the time period in which your chosen character actually "lived" rather than allowing him/her to make commentary on current events or, for that matter, anything that occurred or was invented after the publication year of the story in which s/he appeared.

Give your blog a catchy title and identify who the blogger is. Example:

"It's a Jungle Out There"—by Tarzan

Twenty Questions

From the following list, choose a question that you have a strong opinion about. For the next week, write a 200-word blog each day which supports your answer to the question you picked.

- What influences do we need to protect our children from?
- What piece of movie or theater memorabilia would you most like to own?
- Should funding for the arts come from the government or private donors?
- What environmental issue concerns you the most?
- What will define your 15 minutes of fame?
- What's your opinion of adult offspring living with their parents?
- What new law(s) would you like to make?
- Should every high school graduate pursue a college education?
- What subject do you most appreciate in photography— nature, architecture, people, inanimate objects?
- Do you define people by what they do for a living?
- What three musicians (living or dead) would you most like to have dinner with?
- What culture most intrigues you?
- If you could time-travel, would you go to the past or to the future?
- Do you have confidence in what the media reports?
- What subject do you wish you had studied in school?
- What's the best way to handle stress?
- What talent would you most like to have?
- What is our world's most pressing problem?
- How should children be taught the value of money?
- What piece of technology could you not live without?

Poetic License

Pretend for a moment that you are passionate about movies. So passionate, in fact, that you do a weekly blog on your website which analyzes and reviews your favorite flicks and sometimes even talks about actors whose body of work you especially admire. Whether the movies you choose are classics, art house films, foreign language titles or the latest blockbusters, you are the go-to person for everything related to cinema.

For the next month, you have decided to mix things up a bit for your film-loving fans. Specifically, you are going to write your next four blogs in rhyme.

Example #1:

> Silent movies—what a tease,
> The way we're left to guess.
> All that chatter up on screen,
> Yet all it says is "Yes."
> Damsels fair who swoon and blush,
> Heroes that are buff,
> And always lurking, ever close,
> A villain vile and gruff.

Example #2:

> A wistful gal, a brooding guy
> With skin translucent white.
> What does he mean when first he asks,
> "You want to catch a bite?"
> Can it be he's not from here,
> And lies about his age?
> "Oh pfft!' says Bella, unperturbed.
> "A vampire's all the rage!"

Lyrically Yours

What's that song playing on the radio right now?

If you're listening to a classical station and the only fare is instrumental, please indulge us for a moment and channel-surf until you land on one that plays the latest pop tunes, oldies-but-goodies or Broadway melodies.

Why, you ask?

Back in elementary school when it was too rainy for us to run around outside, I had a teacher who would play a recorded song and then give us 10 minutes to write a short story inspired by what we had just heard. Years later, I *still* use music to jumpstart my imagination, oftentimes musing what the plot would be if a particular song was the signature theme of a motion picture.

Your own assignment takes a similar spin: Compose a one-time blog that transforms existing lyrics into a first-person, 100-word entry. Who knows? It may lead to the start of something much bigger.

Example:

Who says that opposites can't attract?

Most people would tell you I'm a pretty tough, backstreet kind of guy. But last week I saw the most perfect girl I want to marry. Love at first sight! She lives uptown and I know she's used to always having the best of the best. Her mama probably never told her that guys like me even exist, much less that she should ever date one.

But I have dreams. Big dreams. And I just know if I'm patient and let her get to know the real me, she'll tell the world she's mine.

Inspired by Billy Joel's "Uptown Girl"

A Storied Past

When items get handed down through the generations, there's a lot that can get lost in translation … as well as sometimes embellished for the sake of escalating the items' value. In the absence of provenance, who's to say whether the origins are actually based on truth or have become a game of Chinese Whispers (known as "telephone" in the U.S.)? While we like to think we understand and accurately remember every detail told to us about a particular heirloom, those details are shaped by two things: (1) the intentions of the person who initiated the story and (2) the frames of reference of the subsequent listeners.

It's something you often see on programs such as *Antiques Roadshow* when a person proudly declares that the pair of antique scissors she has brought to the appraisal table once belonged to an ancestor who used to be Betsy Ross' neighbor. "One day my ancestor's scissors broke and Betsy said, 'Oh here, please take mine.'" It's a lovely story to be sure, but even if the engraved initials say "BR," how do we know the scissors weren't the property of Belphoebe Rundell? Unless other items of Betsy's were similarly engraved or a letter exists to vet this 18th century transaction, the only thing which can be verified is that the style and metal date from the right era. The current owner may not have known any better but, rather, was seduced by nostalgia and generations of wishful thinking.

For this exercise, you're going to *purposely* obscure the truth and come up with the most seemingly plausible back-story blog about any item in your home that (1) is more than 50 years old and (2) you didn't come by as a family heirloom.

Example:

Item: 1917 typewriter

When Ernest Hemingway was an ambulance driver on the Italian front in World War 1, he bought this typewriter so he could draft short stories and maybe one day even write a novel. The carriage handle is bent from where he threw it against a wall, and a sticky mixture of whiskey and cigar ash have gummed up half of the keys. To replace it, he was given a Corona No. 3 by Hadley Richardson, who became his first of four wives.

Coming to Closure

The other day when my husband was on his way home from running errands, he called to tell me that our neighborhood within-easy-walking-distance Office Max was closing. Although there's another Office Max less than a mile away, this news came as a shock. Whenever something familiar is taken away from us without warning, there's a dizzy, discomfiting moment of wondering how, exactly, we're going to deal with its absence.

Now and again, the same feelings emerge when we discover that a favorite restaurant has gone out of business. When did *that* happen? Wasn't it always crowded with happy diners, ourselves included? Weren't its reviews always stellar? Certainly there was no sign of this closure even being in the works when we were there a few months previous.

Likewise, I had recommended a great eatery in Edinburgh to friends who were visiting Scotland for the first time. We had so thoroughly enjoyed the food, ambiance and engaging servers when we dined there almost 20 years ago that I knew our friends would love it, too. Apparently, though, a lot can happen in 20 years. Maybe if we'd made more trips across the pond our patronage could have kept the doors open.

For this exercise, write a blog about something which has been discontinued and the impact it will now have on your life.

Example:

> *I knew I should have bought multiple pairs when I had the chance. Why is it that whenever you find a pair of jeans that fit perfectly for your weight, height and budget, it is guaranteed the manufacturer will have stopped making them by the time you're ready to make a second purchase? Thus begins a time-wasting quest all over again to go forth and find a different brand. Loyalty to the original makes this a challenge because you can't help but make brutal comparisons. The same goes for lipstick: Buy a single tube in a shade that's a match made in Heaven and it will have completely vanished from the shelves within a month. Could it be that jeans manufacturers and the cosmetics industry are in cahoots to drive us crazy?*

Imaginary Friends

I was an only child growing up and, accordingly, often felt lonely before I was able to start first grade. I remedied this state by having a boatload of imaginary friends—most of whom were named after The Mouseketeers. For hours on end, I'd run around the backyard shouting, "Good one, Annette!" "Watch out, Cubby!" "I'm going inside for lunch, Jimmie, so you're in charge!" "Get off the swing, Sharon! It's my turn!" Even at a young age, I was good at mimicking voices, a talent that on more than one occasion compelled the neighbors to ask my parents, "How many children do you have again?"

Pretend friends are neither uncommon nor, in most cases, are they cause for worry. Studies have shown that children who interact with invisible pals tend to be more creative, engage in abstract thinking, try on different roles, act as their own sounding board in problem-solving, and be able to argue two sides of an issue in mock conversation. Further, it's an early springboard to a future career as a writer and an actor. ("Thank you, my imaginary friends. I could not have had a successful career in both of these without you.")

We have to wonder if famous people in the past had pretend pals to chat with. Edgar Allan Poe, for instance. And what would happen if the imaginary friend thought s/he was the real one and not the reverse? How would it read if s/he wrote a blog about the relationship? That's your assignment this time around.

Example:

How do you tell a friend he really, really needs a vacation? Hanging out with Edgar was fun at the start because he's a great storyteller. "The Tell-Tale Heart" and "The Murders in the Rue Morgue"? Awesome sauce! I also like to think I've been filling an important void after he had that ugly falling out with his folks. They wanted him to go into the family business, manage his money better, stop drinking, yadda yadda yadda but I have to give him credit for sticking to his guns. Lately though—and I don't mean to sound jealous or judgmental—he's been spending more time talking to an imaginary raven instead of me. Can you believe it?! An imaginary birdbrain? From what I hear, it's not even a very good conversationalist.

Room for Improvement

Sometimes when your own writing feels stuck in neutral, an easy way to get out of it is to put on your editor's hat and edit someone else's work.

Since there's no shortage of blogs out there as a starting point, do a Google search on a topic that interests you; i.e., travel blogs, cooking blogs, movie blogs, advice blogs. It's best, however, to stay away from the work of bloggers you know personally or that you know *of*, the reason being it could influence how you approach the task of editing.

Read the blog start-to-finish *without* editing anything to glean an understanding of the blogger's message and level of expertise. On subsequent rounds, peel your eyes for the following:

- ✓ Errors in spelling, grammar, punctuation, verb/subject agreement.
- ✓ Rambling sentences which could be shortened or split in two.
- ✓ Repetitive verbiage.
- ✓ Passive voice.
- ✓ Content which meanders off-message.
- ✓ Long words where a shorter word could be more effective.
- ✓ Excessive adverbs.

If you're new to editing, there's a free online app you may find helpful. The Hemingway Editor (http://www.hemingwayapp.com) is a color-coded tool which doesn't just identify the readability of the text; it also offers suggestions on how to improve it.

Another fun editing exercise when you copy and paste the original blog into a Word document is to make note of the word count. Whatever it is, strive to trim it down by at least two-thirds. In my online writing classes, for instance, one of the most popular challenges is to edit Lincoln's Gettysburg Address (272 words) by half without losing any of the context.

CHAPTER 3
HE SAID, SHE SAID

In case you haven't noticed (and how long have you been on this planet?), males and females often convey the same information in completely different styles.

For men, the purpose of communication is to exchange information in the form of facts and figures. In contrast, women view talking as a way to forge new relationships and nurture existing ones. As psychologists explain it, women are capable of thinking and feeling at the same time. Most men, however, can think *or* feel but not simultaneously. Studies published by *Psychology Today* and *The Journal of Neuroscience* further cite that women can speak at 250 words per minute while men can speak at only 125. Is it any wonder that husbands often feel out-talked by their wives or that getting a word in edgewise is not unlike trying to thread a sewing machine while it's running?

If you want to improve your dialogue-writing skills for works of fiction, the exercises in this chapter will be of enormous help. Before you get started, though, let's warm up with one paragraph each on the following questions:

- Who do you think tells better jokes—males or females?
- Who do you think gives better political speeches—males or females?
- Who do you think delivers better eulogies—males or females?
- If you were a detective at a crime scene and you had two witnesses of the opposite sex, which one do you think would supply a greater level of detail?
- Do you think it's easier for a male to write in a female "voice" or a female to write in a male "voice?"
- If you were asked to look at a piece of writing and were not told the gender of the author, what clues would you look for to decipher whether it was written by a male or a female? If you found out the authorship was the opposite of what you assumed, would it influence your reaction to the content?

Into the Woods

With the exception of *Snow White* where the evil queen spends a lot of face time with her talking mirror, fairy tales are written from the viewpoint of the leading character. We generally don't know the back-stories, hopes, dreams, fears, etc. of the supporting players because they functionally serve as props to keep the action moving forward for the protagonist and/or tie everything up neatly as a happily ever after.

But what if we were to get inside the heads of these other characters and allow them to explain things from their own perspectives?

What if, for instance, it wasn't a coincidence the woodsman just happened to stroll near the cottage in time to save Red Riding Hood and her grandmother? What if he was besotted with Red's older sister and had been trying the past few weeks to get up the nerve to ask Red if her sister was dating anyone? What if the elves who helped the shoemaker were in the witness protection program and this was the easiest cottage to hang out after dark? Or what if the giant who lived in the castle atop Jack's beanstalk was a reclusive novelist who just liked having his privacy so he could be at his most creative?

Your assignment: Choose any fairy tale and rewrite it from a minor character's first-person point of view.

Example:

Why does the kid always come in the afternoon when I'm watching my favorite soaps? It's not like I have TiVo and can watch whenever I want. Yeah, she's my granddaughter and some of my friends have family that never visit at all. Do I sound like I'm complaining? I know, I know. I should be grateful she hasn't forgotten me and that she always brings a basket of baked goods but why-oh-why are they always gluten-free, sugar-free and totally tasteless? What ever happened to a nice chocolate cake? Or a pie? A pie would be nice. Maybe something in apple. Wait a minute. There's a knock on the door. Hmmm. Too early to be the kid. I probably shouldn't open it but it might be someone interesting. Maybe UPS. I ordered a new recliner for when I watch my soaps.

What Would Ashley Say?

In 1939, *Gone With the Wind*'s Scarlett O'Hara raised her fist to the sky and angrily swore that—no matter what she had to do—she would never go hungry again. How would the verbiage and delivery of that famous speech be different if reframed from the viewpoint of the soft-spoken Ashley Wilkes, his gentle wife Melanie, or the rakish Rhett Butler? Your assignment: Go to the Best Film Speeches and Monologues website (http://www.filmsite.org/bestspeeches.html) and choose any speech that really resonates with you. Your task is to give this speech or monologue to the opposite sex and rewrite the content. Here are some starters:

I don't know if you'd be particularly interested in hearing anything about me, my life, I mean. Most of it doesn't add up to much that I could relate as a way of life that you'd approve of. I move around a lot. Not because I'm looking for anything, really, but — 'cause I'm getting away from things that get bad if I stay. Auspicious beginnings. You know what I mean? **(Jack Nicholson, Five Easy Pieces)**

I am packing my belongings in the shawl my mother used to wear when she went to the market. And I'm going from my valley. And this time, I shall never return. I am leaving behind me my fifty years of memory. Memory. Streams that the mind will forget so much of what only this moment has passed, and yet hold clear and bright the memory of what happened years ago – of men and women long since dead. Yet who shall say what is real and what is not? **(Roddy McDowall, How Green Was My Valley)**

I woke up this morning, kept thinking about Billy and I was thinking about him waking up in his room with his little clouds all around that I painted. And I thought I should have painted clouds downtown, because then he would think that he was waking up at home. I came here to take my son home. And I realized he already is home. **(Meryl Streep, Kramer vs. Kramer)**

Hopper, what's the matter with you? You gotta be crazy chasin' me halfway across the country. Why are you doin' this to me? ...You know, well, I've got a dream too. But it's about singing and dancing and making people happy. That's the kind of dream that gets better the more people you share it with. And, well, I've found a whole bunch of friends who have the same dream. And, and it kind of makes us like a family. You have anybody like that, Hopper? I mean, once you get all those restaurants, who are you gonna share it with? **(Kermit, The Muppet Movie)**

Rehearsing on Paper

Whenever she was faced with a difficult conversation, a friend of mine used to say it would be so much easier if she could just write it out on a piece of paper and hand it to the other party instead of having to say anything out loud. That way, she said, she wouldn't have to worry about leaving out something important or inadvertently saying/promising something off-the-cuff which could later come back to haunt her.

For each of the following scenarios, write a one-paragraph "rehearsal speech." As an extra challenge, *rewrite* each of them but in the voice of the opposite sex.

- A woman in her 50s tells her husband she wants to go back to college.
- A man finds his estranged sibling through social media and wants to reconnect.
- A former child star wants a studio head to facilitate a come-back.
- A student dropping out of school wants to explain why a job in the circus is more important.
- An employee passed over for promotion wants a reconsideration.
- A neighbor confronts a local gossip.
- An actor contests a critic's scathing review.
- A woman wins a lunch date with her favorite TV star.
- A spouse seeks forgiveness and a second chance at love.
- An entrepreneur tries to convince a small town it needs to establish a youth theatre.
- A father wants to explain to his teenage offspring why he is remarrying.
- A mother wants to explain to her teenage offspring why she is divorcing.

Getting Emotional

Storytellers and filmmakers have a long history of using anthropomorphism to ascribe human traits to non-human entities. Whether it's talking animals in *An American Tail, Babe, Ice Age, The Lion King* and *Finding Nemo*, the enchanted objects in *Beauty and the Beast*, or Woody and Buzz in *Toy Story*, the purpose is to show we're not all that different when it comes to wanting to feel safe, loved and appreciated.

In the 2015 animated movie, *Inside Out*, anthropomorphism goes a step more in showing how emotions themselves—specifically, Joy, Fear, Anger, Sadness and Disgust—are their own unique personalities living inside a little girl's head.

For each of the following scenarios, write a two-paragraph monologue in which each of the five "voices" referenced above reacts to the same situation. Write them a second time as the opposite gender.

1) The end of a relationship.
2) A move to a different city.
3) The loss of a job.
4) An outcome in an election.
5) The discovery of a family secret.
6) A journey to a different country.

Example of opening lines for Scenario #3:

Yay! No more getting up at 3am for a job that bored me out of my socks.

I've never been unemployed in my life. How can I possibly support myself and put food on the table?

What a jerk to fire me for no reason! Does he not know who he's dealing with? Mark my words—I'm not leaving quietly!

I can't stop crying. That job was the best thing that ever happened to me and now it's gone forever.

Typical bureaucracy! It's no skin off their nose to short-change workers, fire them at will and then label the whole thing "progress."

Getting To Know You

For this writing exercise, you're the social director of an eclectic club and it's your job to write up scintillating profiles of the club's members for inclusion in upcoming issues of the newsletter. These profiles are 100 words and cover such things as where they're from, what they do for a living, family life, and what makes them unique.

The first part of the assignment is to pick four occupations from the following random list. Before you start writing, though, the second instruction is to flip a coin which will determine if each of the individuals you're writing about is male or female.

Postal worker
Combat pilot
Psychic
Film director
Chauffeur
Sketch artist
Shopkeeper
Bodyguard
Circus performer
Mechanic
Gospel singer
Archaeologist
Ballet dancer
Park ranger
Wedding planner
Mystery writer

Example: *Denny Duffy took so many tumbles growing up in his native Kennebunkport, Maine, that by the time he turned 25, he figured he had no more bones left to break. He and his high school sweetheart, Lenore, and their four kids headed out to Hollywood where he quickly became the highest paid stunt person and body double for the studios' leading action stars. So what scares him the most? "Absolutely nothing," Denny replies. Blind since birth, he relates, "There's nothing that can freak me out if I can't even see it coming."*

The Color of the Sky

Who knew there were so many different shades of white? Years ago I went to a fabric store in San Francisco with my matron of honor. Our quest was to find some white satin and lace to make a detachable train for my wedding dress. Wisely, she suggested we take the dress along with us rather than try to guess the right shade for a perfect match. When we entered the store, I was amazed to discover an entire wall filled with bolts of white fabric ... and no two exactly the same! *Ecru, eggshell, ivory, moonstone, lily, snow.* To an unpracticed eye, they all met the definition of whiteness and yet could have been disastrous choices if we hadn't been able to hold the dress up to each one for comparison.

Interestingly, men and women are different when it comes to distinguishing subtleties in hue and saturation. According to neuroscience studies published in an article for Smithsonian (https://www.smithsonianmag.com/science-nature/where-men-see-white-women-see-ecru-22540446/), females are better at discriminating gradations in the middle of the color spectrum. Females also have a larger vocabulary for describing the colors they see—no doubt a product of buying nail polish and eye shadows with names such as Napa Grape, Jazz Club, Summer Orange, Blue Lagoon, Gatsby Pink, Bordeaux Lust, and Sandcastle.

Your assignment: Pick a color from the list below, set a timer for 10 minutes, and write down as many descriptors as you can come up with.

Example for **Red**: *brick, cherry, crimson, fire-engine.*

Black
Grey
Green
Red
Blue
White
Yellow
Brown
Purple

Casting Call

Whenever I'm working on a new novel or script, I often find it helpful to play casting director in my head and imagine favorite actors in the various roles. This helps me to "hear" how they talk as well as imagine how they'd dress and the way they move.

For this exercise, make a list of your six favorite performers in television or film—three female and three male. The next step is to choose one of the following story set-ups:

- ✓ A technician in a remote mental hospital discovers a famous celebrity is being held against his/her will.
- ✓ Six months before his ex-wife's wedding, a man decides to reinvent himself and win her back.
- ✓ A journalist discovers a philanthropist has been diverting funds for personal reasons that are tragic.
- ✓ A shy employee finally makes her/his move on a secret office crush.
- ✓ A farmer discovers that his/her crops have grown to astonishing proportions following a meteor shower the previous night. The spouse has a theory.
- ✓ A nanny in Central Park is approached by a stranger with a mysterious request.
- ✓ A popular talk-show psychic awakens one morning to discover his/her powers no longer exist. Only one other person is aware of this unsettling news.
- ✓ At their 30th high school reunion, two attendees decide to meet for drinks and revisit why their past dreams didn't work out.

Based on the scenario you choose, cast your two leading actors and write a one-page synopsis of where you would take the storyline.

Consider how the storyline would be different if you subsequently re-cast it with the other actors on your list.

To Fib Or Not To Fib

Although Shakespeare's play *Cardenio* was performed during his lifetime, it was never recorded in the First Folio of 1623 along with his other works. Is the original manuscript collecting dust in the back of a closet? Did it get left on public transportation on the way to the printers? Was Will short on cash one day for his pub tab at the Fox and Goose and left the manuscript as collateral?

This is a one page memo-to-self exercise which is written first in a male voice and then in a female voice. How do men and women differ when it comes to decision-making? According to a May 2016 interview with Dr. Therese Huston in *Forbes*, men are more eager to gamble and take risks when they're under stress, even if the outcome of a high-stakes reward is iffy. In contrast, women are more alert to risks and focus on smaller wins that carry a higher guarantee of success.

Keep this in mind with the following scenario:

> You are a struggling playwright on holiday in London who happens across what looks to be the missing script at an antique shop. Will you choose to (1) pass the script off as your own work, (2) cast and direct the "lost" production, (3) start a bidding war among private collectors, or (4) donate it to a museum. Identify your obstacles and adversaries as well as the motivations for whichever choice is pursued.

CHAPTER 4
ROOM WITH A VIEW

"A man's home is his castle" says an old English proverb. But who's to say how loosely "castle" is defined?

Back in the 1990s, I was writing romantic suspense novels for HarperCollins and one of my plots was set in the Hawaiian Islands. My boss at the time had been born and raised on Oahu and spent most of her formative years in an orphanage run by nuns. I wanted authenticity in my novel and decided she'd be a great resource insofar as identifying where the wealthy heroine and her in-laws might live.

"Oh, no question," she replied. "It would be such-and-such." She described how the beautiful homes were built on a mountain that overlooked the Pacific and how the road leading up to the estates occupied by rich people was flanked by towering banyan trees. As it turned out, I was planning a trip to Oahu later that year and was excited to see this enclave of fabulous homes she had so enthusiastically described.

When I got there—following her directions—I saw the banyan trees standing like noble sentries. What lay beyond, however, was a smattering of Depression-era stucco cottages and wood sheds woefully in need of repair work. I checked and rechecked the address. I asked some of the local merchants, still believing I had somehow missed a turn. Nope. That was it. How could she have misunderstood what I said when I'd asked her where the wealthy people might call home?

And then I realized she'd spoken the truth, the truth of an adolescent who had grown up with so little. Perhaps she spent a lot of time wistfully looking up at the mountain and being told this was the place where islanders who were "well off" happened to reside. Maybe it was even the nuns who emphasized the message that if one was living in Paradise, such existence was already considered priceless.

The exercises in this section are all about being on the outside looking in...and being on the inside looking out. It's all a matter of perception and frame of reference that defines a home's value and comfort level.

Where You Hang Your Hat

"It takes hands to build a house," wrote an unknown author, "but only hearts can build a home."

Whether it's a tiny space, a humongous mansion or anything in-between, what happens within the walls and beneath the roof of the place you call home not only help to shape your identity and your goals but also provide you with memories—good and bad—to be carried for a lifetime.

Write a one paragraph answer to each of the following questions:

- Do you currently live in an apartment, a condominium, a duplex or a house?
- If you were describing your home to a stranger in 25 words or less, what would you say?
- How many people do you live with? Are there any pets?
- Do you have a backyard? If so, what is your favorite thing to do there?
- What's your favorite room where you live and why?
- If you could design your own home (and money wasn't an object), where would it be and what would it look like?
- Would you prefer a home in a big city, a small town, a forest, by the ocean, in the desert or in the mountains?
- Do you know your neighbors?
- When you moved away from home and into your first place, was it to live alone or with roommates?
- How many times have you moved thus far in your life? How many good experiences versus bad experiences?

Who Lives Here?

I've loved architecture for as long as I can remember. In fact, I still have a habit harkening back to childhood in which I like to make up stories about the people who occupy an eclectic mix of dwellings. Now it's your turn to do the same thing by writing short character sketches about the owners of each of the following:

The Unexpected Visitor

Using one of the settings in the previous exercise, write a one-page scene in which the person you have identified as being the owner comes home to the discovery of a guest that s/he was not expecting.

The scene can be written as the start of a short story, novel, theatrical script or screenplay and can be any genre of your choosing (comedy, drama, horror, science fiction, romance, western, supernatural, etc.).

As an additional challenge, rewrite the scene and change the gender of the two characters.

The Roomies

In a wobbly economy, homeowners are sometimes forced to take in boarders or even to house-share if it means being able to hold on to their property until things start looking better.

For your next story starter, take a look at the American Film Institute's list of the 100 Greatest Villains and Heroes (http://www.filmsite.org/afi100heroesvilla.html). Make the most quirky pairing you can think of, decide what kind of place these two will share (including where it's located), and how they'll divide the chores.

Examples:

George Bailey and Michael Corleone
Ellen Ripley and Nurse Ratched
Detective Harry Callahan and Gordon Gekko
Obi-Wan Kenobi and HAL 9000
Norma Rae and Mrs. Danvers
Philip Marlowe and Count Dracula
Clarice Starling and Cruella DeVil
Rooster Cogburn and Hans Gruber

The Boxes

When people divorce, they sometimes do silly things just out of spite. My first husband and I had a particularly ugly split which led to several episodes of stealing wedding presents back and forth when the other wasn't looking. On the day I recruited some friends to help me move furniture, I recalled that there were half a dozen taped-up archive boxes of his that had been sitting in the garage ever since we'd bought the house three years previous. I had no idea what was in them but I instructed my friends to scoop them up and bring them along.

In the weeks that followed, I full expected him to call me and demand their return. Time passed. He didn't call. I didn't open them. Some more time passed and the boxes were not only pushed farther back in the closet but also farther back in my memory. Several moves later, I was still having them moved as if they were my own and that one day I'd get around to seeing what was inside.

It wasn't until my beloved and I were preparing to move to Southern California in 2002 that he asked me what was in the boxes stashed under the stairwell. I confessed that (1) I had no idea, (2) they were my ex's and (3) I had taken them in 1982.

Common sense prevailed that we weren't paying the movers to take them *anywhere* unless we determined what was inside.

Your assignment for this time around is to put yourself in the same situation and identify:

- ✓ What is in the boxes?
- ✓ What's your reaction to it?
- ✓ Is it valuable or is it junk?
- ✓ If it's valuable, would you feel inclined to apologize and return it?
- ✓ Would the contents in any way cause you to change your feelings toward the actual owner?

Okay, so after a set-up like that, you're probably curious as to what I had been schlepping around from one address to the next for 20 years. Let's just say he was as devious as I was and tricked me into helping him declutter his garage.

Home Again

A friend of mine recently found himself on a business trip to the city where he and his siblings grew up. Although the family moved across the country before any of them were out of elementary school, he wondered what the old neighborhood looked like. Even more importantly, he wondered if he could trust his memory to drive around and find their old house. It actually took him three drives around the block until he realized he'd already found it.

"To be honest," he said, "I was looking for a place that was much bigger."

When you're little, you view things from a much different perspective, including the size of the yard and the height of the trees. Unless you return to a place on a regular basis (i.e., Grandma's house for the holidays), the differences between memory and reality can be staggering ... even if the place itself has never physically changed.

For this writing exercise, sit in a quiet place where you can reflect. Take a mental tour of your childhood home. Room by room— starting with the front door—write down on a piece of paper every detail you can remember.

Things to consider:
- ✓ Paint color/wallpaper patterns
- ✓ Carpet/tile/wood
- ✓ Curtains/blinds/shutters
- ✓ Furniture fabrics and colors
- ✓ How many windows and what was the view?
- ✓ Largest piece of furniture in the room
- ✓ Smallest piece of furniture in the room
- ✓ What was hanging on the walls?
- ✓ Best memory the room holds for you
- ✓ Type of yard
- ✓ Carport/garage
- ✓ Was there an attic? A basement?
- ✓ Outside sounds heard through an open window
- ✓ What season did your childhood home look best in?
- ✓ What season did your childhood home look worst in?
- ✓ How was it decorated for holidays and special occasions?

Changing the Locks

One of my colleagues grew up in a military family that moved a lot. In fact, he had already lived in nine different countries by the time he graduated from high school.

While it was an upbringing that gave him an appreciation of other cultures and introduced him to foreign languages that he still uses on his travels, I remember him saying that the biggest fear he had as a kid was that he'd come home from school one day and discover his family had packed up and moved somewhere without him. His fears ran the gamut of whether he'd completely forgotten it was moving day to whether it was an April Fool's prank to whether his parents thought raising four sons was too much work and he was the expendable one.

Let's put yourself in the same scenario but as an adult and under the following conditions:

- You don't have a cell phone, pager or laptop with you. In other words, no accessible technology.
- You lost your wallet and, hence, your ID.
- You forgot where you had parked your car.
- You did, however, have just enough change in your pockets to take a bus ride and walk a few blocks to your house.
- The neighborhood looks exactly the same as the last time you saw it but no one appears to be around.
- You put your key in the lock but it doesn't work.
- The door is opened by someone you don't know who claims that s/he has lived there for over 20 years.

Your assignment:

Make a list of 10 things you would try to do to (1) prove your identity and (2) find out what happened in the interim since you left that morning. Turn it into a short story that serves up an explanation. Whether or not that explanation is plausible is up to you.

Possessions

As of this writing, the newspapers have carried no shortage of heartbreaking stories about individuals that have lost their homes to flooding, earthquakes and massive fires. It's not just the loss of a physical structure, though, but the years of memories—and possessions—that went into making every house a true home.

The writer's block exercises on this page can be as short as a few words or as long a few paragraphs. The important thing is that the answers you supply may trigger a remembrance you hadn't thought about for years ... and may now want to develop as an introspective essay or the start of a new story.

- The first thing you ever remember breaking, whether by accident or on purpose.
- The most recent possession you gave away, why and to whom.
- Three things that have outlived their usefulness but are too nostalgic for you to discard.
- Possessions that remind you of where you came from.
- Possessions that remind you of where you'd like to be.
- The most recent thing you sold and for how much.
- Possessions you have more than one of.
- Things you have recycled or turned into something different.
- Aside from family members and pets, identify the one thing you couldn't leave behind in a disaster.
- Three items in your possession that are irreplaceable.
- The oldest, strangest or most nostalgic item in your closet at this moment.
- What happened to your childhood toys?
- A possession you've lost that you'd really like to have back.

CHAPTER 5
ME, MYSELF AND I

Have you ever kept a diary? In my tween and teen years, it was all the rage to record one's daily thoughts in a 4x6" pastel journal that locked with the tiniest little key. Within its lined pages, I'd mince no commentary about how much I hated gym class, lament that my latest crush wasn't paying me any notice, and vow that I would never, ever again talk to my best friend over a slight which—more often than not—had a shelf life of about three days and was subsequently forgotten.

I committed my craziest dreams, my fondest hopes, my most terrifying fears and all the angst inherent in growing up to a dutifully locked journal which I trusted was for my eyes only. Respect for my privacy, however, was never a priority in my mother's world. Not only did she routinely pick the lock (okay, let's be honest, a squirrel with a hatpin could have picked it) but she'd regale her cocktail-swilling friends with all of the "silly" entries she had read.

Once I found out about this, I decided that no place in the world could be safe from prying eyes if I intended to keep my innermost thoughts my own. While I stopped keeping a journal per se (even after I moved away and into my first apartment), I did find a way to continue to examine feelings, to memorialize fears and regrets, and to give my remembrance of conversations a sustainable platform:

I turn the truth into [sometimes] thinly disguised works of fiction.

I also know I'm not alone in this approach. Many an author I have interviewed* has said s/he embroiders personal experiences into the fabric of their plots and imbues the protagonists and villains with aspects of their own personalities. Why else would these emotions and characters feel so real were it not for the fact they were already alive long before they were ever committed to paper?

This chapter is all about how to use self-reflection and role-playing as a powerful story-starter tool.

You Read It Here First (fromtheauthors.wordpress.com)

Tell Me About Yourself

We've probably all been in the situation of walking into a job interview and hearing, "So ... tell me about yourself" as the very first question. Isn't your letter of introduction and your resume sitting right under the interviewer's nose? Is this some kind of a quirky quiz to see if you actually *know* what's on your resume? Or is it the fact that a lot of people simply don't like talking about themselves, much less tooting their own horn?

In this role-playing exercise, choose a famous person from the following list, research his/her accomplishments, and then write a first-person paragraph in answer to an interviewer's tell-me-about-yourself question.

- ✓ Winston Churchill
- ✓ Mother Teresa
- ✓ Queen Victoria
- ✓ Abraham Lincoln
- ✓ Jane Austen
- ✓ Martin Luther King
- ✓ J.M. Barrie
- ✓ Nefertiti
- ✓ Albert Einstein
- ✓ Amelia Earhart
- ✓ Jesse Owens
- ✓ Nelly Bly
- ✓ William Shakespeare
- ✓ Gertrude Ederle
- ✓ Mark Twain
- ✓ Frances Perkins
- ✓ Alexander Graham Bell
- ✓ Eleanor of Aquitaine

After you've successfully occupied the head of one of these luminaries, the second challenge in this exercise is to write an introductory paragraph about ... You.

It's All Relative

As the saying goes, you can choose your friends and you can choose the person you marry but you have no control over choosing your own family. Except, in this case, you actually do.

Reflect a moment on some of your favorite television shows which were all about family interactions. Here's a starter list to jog your memory:

Family Ties
The Waltons
Leave It to Beaver
Gilmore Girls
Family Matters
Eight Is Enough
Ozzie and Harriet
Modern Family
Parenthood
Family Affair
The Munsters
Growing Pains
Fresh Prince of Bel Air
Full House
The Wonder Years
The Addams Family
The Simpsons
Everybody Loves Raymond
The Partridge Family
The Brady Bunch
Malcolm in the Middle
Little House on the Prairie

If you could live with any of these fictional families for a week, who would it be? Who would you most like to have as your dad? Your mom? Your siblings? For each of your answers, provide a one paragraph why.

Coulda/Woulda/Shoulda

When you reach your twilight years, what are you going to look back on and perhaps wish you had done differently? But hey, why wait until then to reflect on missed opportunities, chance encounters, hasty decisions, awkward revelations, and moments that you wish came with a do-over button.

Write a one-sentence response to each of the following questions, then use that sentence as the opening line of some flash fiction, a short story, a personal blog or a novel.

- ✓ What should I have known about my family that no one wanted to tell me?
- ✓ What do I most regret saying to someone I cared about?
- ✓ At what moment did I realize I'd made a mistake in my career choice?
- ✓ What do I daydream about the most?
- ✓ When I was 10, who did I most want to trade places with?
- ✓ What do I wish I had learned to do but never took the time or had the chance?
- ✓ When did I have the time of my life?
- ✓ What conversation would I most like to rewind and start over?
- ✓ If it were possible, what age would I like to be forever?
- ✓ Whose companion do I miss the most?
- ✓ What was the most pivotal point in my life?
- ✓ How would my best friend describe me?
- ✓ How would my worst enemy describe me?
- ✓ When have I felt the most lost?
- ✓ How is my current different from what I imagined it would be?
- ✓ Was there a time when I wish I had gotten involved?
- ✓ Was there a time when I wish I had left a situation sooner?
- ✓ What do I try the hardest to avoid because of memories it conjures?
- ✓ Have I ever received a wake-up call to make a dramatic change in my life or lifestyle?

Keeping Resolutions

January 1st has a longstanding tradition of being the date everyone equates with a clean slate, a fresh start, a commitment to reinvention. While over half the population makes resolutions, 22 percent fail in the first week, 40 percent after one month, and 60 percent after six months.

It's not that they didn't have good intentions. Most of the time it's just a matter of not having a clearly defined goal to begin with, not creating an action plan to implement it, or setting an unreasonable expectation and then becoming frustrated when it's not being met overnight.

The following questions are all about the self-improvement promises we make … and the challenges of seeing them through. Use your answers as the start of an article or blog.

- ✓ Do you make New Year's resolutions? Why or why not?
- ✓ If there was no risk of failure, what would you resolve to change about your life as it is now?
- ✓ What was the most recent resolution you made? Were you successful at keeping it? If yes, what were the influences? If no, what were the obstacles?
- ✓ Do you think it's harder to break a bad habit or to incorporate a good habit into your behavior?
- ✓ Should you tell anyone what your New Year's resolutions are or just quietly keep them to yourself?
- ✓ If you had all of the support you needed to steadfastly keep to the code of a resolution, what is it you would most like to change about yourself? In what way do you think that a change in yourself (i.e., losing a substantial amount of weight) would impact your relationships with others?
- ✓ Do you ever toss coins in wishing wells?
- ✓ What are some ways people could/should reward themselves for the discipline of maintaining a bold new reinvention plan?

Letter to Myself

When I was around 10, I carefully composed a list of all the qualities I wanted to someday find in a husband. That list mysteriously disappeared a few months later. (I suspect the same person who broke into my diary had something to do with this.)

Although I don't remember *everything* on that long ago list, I managed to retain a few of them as being Really Important:

- Must love animals (especially dogs).
- Must speak foreign languages.
- Must be able to sing.
- Must be able to do funny impressions and make me laugh.
- Must be kind.
- Must be very smart and like to read books.
- Must be in the Navy.

Those who know my beloved husband can attest my wish list was uncannily accurate. Even at such a young age, I knew who I'd want to spend the rest of my life with. Maybe a guardian angel from the future was whispering in my ear ...

What advice would you give to your own younger self based on the lessons you've learned and the experiences you've had?

Ruminate on this in a quiet place, then compose a one-page letter to your adolescent or teen self. And tempting as it may be to include advice such as, "Purchase stock in a new company called Amazon" or "Buy property on Katella Avenue in Anaheim, California because Disneyland will give you a boatload of money to sell it to them for their theme park expansion," the object of this exercise is to reflect on the people who had your best interests at heart ("Listen to your Uncle Saul"), to dissuade unhealthy habits ("Cigarettes won't do your lungs any favors"), and to pay attention to small things that can lead to huge things ("Help someone without any expectation of your kindness being repaid").

Decisions, Decisions

On any day of the week, we're asked to make decisions. Some of them are small decisions: Should I have a bowl of Wheaties™ or Cheerios™ for my breakfast? Should I get my hair cut this weekend or can it wait until the end of the month? Should I drive my car today or take the bus?

Others are major decisions that will have significant impact on our lives and relationships: Should I quit my job and become a full-time musician? Should I get married? Should I get divorced? Should I offload all of my possessions and move to Bratislava?

How a decision is made is based on several factors; i.e., age, gender, social status, education, prior experience and personal support network. Consider each of the following scenarios and write a three-sentence answer explaining your choice.

Are you more likely to give money to a well-dressed stranger who says his wallet was stolen or a shabbily dressed homeless person who says he's hungry?

If the costs were comparable, would you bring an ailing relative home to live with you the rest of their life or find a nursing facility to take care of them?

If you knew you'd be completely vindicated in three years for whistle-blowing at your place of business, would losing your job and reputation be worth it?

Which of the following would you choose to prevent if you had the power—a tsunami that kills 50,000 people, a train wreck that kills 300 people, or a car accident that claims the life of a close acquaintance?

Would you rather have the power to become invisible or to read people's minds?

Would you accept a boring job that paid three times more and had higher benefits than a low-paying job you enjoy doing?

Would you rather live in an environment that is always swelteringly hot or bitterly cold?

If you were the only witness to an assault, would you get involved and try to save the victim?

Bad Fit Fads

Oh, the drama of being a teenager and attempting to keep up with the latest labels that define "cool." It's a fragile age when one is desperately trying to individuate and yet just as zealously wants to imitate whatever trend the "In" crowd is either following or establishing.

I look back on pictures of myself in high school and am pretty sure that white *Hullabaloo* go-go boots, mini-skirts with paisley blouses, turquoise eyeshadow, pale lipstick, bellbottom pants, and big hair worn in a Marlo Thomas flip were probably not fashion statements I came up with on my own.

Every generation can find something amusing about how prior generations dressed themselves. (Seriously, did *anyone* think that men's pastel polyester leisure suits with white shoes were a smart idea?) Future generations will probably look back at us and ask, "What were they thinking?"

For this exercise, identify two fads from your past—one of which was actually a great idea that is still in vogue and the other a bad fit fad you're embarrassed to admit was a band wagon you jumped on. Write a paragraph about each one and what the fad represented to you at the time.

Now it's *your* turn to come up with a new fad. The sillier, the better.

Here are some ideas to get you started:

- Fascinators will be worn in the workplace by all employees (including men).
- Pet Buttons will become the new Pet Rocks.
- Custom Pez™ dispensers will be hood ornaments for cars.
- Take Your Grandmother To Work Day.
- Tie Dye wedding dresses with Mood ring earrings.

A Matter of Faith

For each of the following questions, use your answer as the opening paragraph of a personal blog.

- ✓ Is there a difference between religion and spirituality?
- ✓ Have you ever experienced something that could only be described as a miracle?
- ✓ Who or what have you prayed for most recently?
- ✓ If a stranger told you s/he was your guardian angel, what would your reaction be?
- ✓ Have you ever felt you have lived a previous life?
- ✓ Do you read your horoscope every morning?
- ✓ Are you superstitious?
- ✓ Would you date or marry someone of a different faith than yours?
- ✓ Why do bad things happen to good people?
- ✓ Do you believe in free will or predestination?
- ✓ Have you ever taken a leap of faith?
- ✓ Are you more or less spiritual than you were 10 years ago?
- ✓ Can fortunetellers predict the future?
- ✓ Do you believe in good luck charms?
- ✓ Have you ever questioned or lost your faith?
- ✓ Do you ever worry about where you'll go when you're no longer here?
- ✓ Do you believe in déjà vu?
- ✓ What do you believe your purpose or true calling is?

CHAPTER 6
1 PICTURE=1,000 WORDS

What do you do with a bunch of restless fifth graders on a rainy day? My English teacher had a solution which so clicked in my imagination that I still use it all these years later. Specifically, she'd tape a wide variety of pictures on the chalkboard. Some of them depicted famous works of art such as Vermeer's *Woman in Blue Reading a Letter* or Rockwell's *Freedom From Want*. Others were pages from vintage calendars or advertisements torn from magazines.

Our job as young wordsmiths was to choose a picture that "spoke" to us and compose a short story about it. We gave names to the people pictured, determined what their relationships were to each other, what they were talking about, what they had for lunch, what sort of houses they lived in, etc. Even though she'd call time at 15 minutes, yours truly was usually the one who was still scribbling away, oblivious to everything around me. Oftentimes, I'd still be thinking about those images weeks later, adding bits and pieces to flesh out whatever story I had begun on that rainy day. Apparently I *still* think about it. Why else would I remember I named the dog in Wyeth's *Master Bedroom* "Mattie" and said she was waiting for young Sarah to return from boarding school in Connecticut and play with her. Alas, but Sarah is in a hospital recovering from pneumonia. Oh no!

Whether it's a photograph, painting, poster, postcard, sculpture or something that simply catches your eye in a travel brochure, use it as the framework for your next story. Decipher the subjects' facial expressions and body language. Speculate about where they buy their clothes and what kind of jobs they hold. Let your mind wander beyond the thick doors and lighted windows of rustic cottages and imagine the people living there. Does the landscape suggest they're at peace with the world … or engaged in battle against it? If the subjects are in a business environment, what do you suppose their email passwords are … and what are some of the websites they have bookmarked? Is one of them holding a cell phone? What's the ringtone of his/her most important contact … and is that the person who's going to call next?

Seriously. Don't get me started.

53

Fine Dining

In 1916, photographer James VanDerZee opened a studio in Harlem and proceeded to capture on film the workaday lives of its African American community. One such photograph was the Manhattan Temple Bible Club's lunchroom, a place where patrons—including single ladies—could enjoy a stylish meal at a modest price.

Your assignment: Assign names and relationships to the three ladies in front of the lunchroom. Along with the faces visible through the window, they all appear to be waiting for someone's arrival. Is it a relative? A customer? A celebrity? An agent of the IRS? Using this tableau as your opening scene, write the first three pages of a story involving these characters and the individual that shows up.

Having Our Say

In 1943, The Saturday Evening Post published the first of four "freedom" paintings by Norman Rockwell. His inspiration for the images came from a speech written by President Franklin D. Roosevelt. The painting below is called *Freedom of Speech* and reflects Rockwell's remembrance of a town hall meeting he once attended in Vermont.

Your assignment: You're a documentary filmmaker who has heard that a controversial topic is on the agenda for the next town hall gathering. You learn that the man standing in this painting is a key speaker and you want to build your documentary around why he has decided to speak up. Develop a one-page proposal in which you (1) identify the topic, (2) determine whether he is for or against this topic (and why), and (3) decide what kind of imagery and interviews you would incorporate in your documentary to make this a compelling show for viewers.

They've Got a Secret

In this painting by American artist Edward Hopper (1882-1967), we see four people at a Manhattan restaurant. One of them has a secret which—when revealed—will change the life of one of the other three. Is it the cashier? Is it the lady arranging items on the table? What about the couple in the corner?

Your assignment: Assign names to the people in this painting and create brief character profiles for them including such things as where they live, whether they have families, and why they're in New York. Give thought to the secret-keeper's motivations for breaking silence on this particular day, then write a two-page scene in which the truth is revealed and those who are present respectively react to it.

Roadside Curiosities

Before the advent of camera phones, I'd see something quirky or weird in an unexpected place and immediately regret that I didn't have a way to capture a picture of it outside my own head.

Nowadays, we don't have any excuse for letting these odd moments slip away.

How long has this pair of weathered suitcases been propped against a tree on a street in suburbia? Who left them there? What do they contain? Could it be the sum total of someone's earthly possessions ... or possessions stolen from someone else and abandoned during pursuit by the police? Does the owner of these suitcases plan to come back for them? What if they contain explosives that will go off if the luggage is opened?

Your assignment: Write a flash fiction story of 300 words or less that explores these very questions.

I'm Thinking, I'm Thinking

Auguste Rodin's famous bronze and marble sculpture of a male in deep contemplation was originally called "The Poet." It was then changed to "The Thinker" and has prompted observers for over a century to speculate what sort of weighty thoughts might be consuming his attention.

According to the artist himself, "What makes my Thinker think is that he thinks not only with his brain, with his knitted brow, his distended nostrils and compressed lips, but with every muscle of his arms, back and legs, with his clenched fist and gripping toes."

Could he be wondering where he left his car keys? Why his pizza hasn't arrived yet? What sort of excuse to give his girlfriend about forgetting her birthday?

Your assignment: Construct a half-page monologue that clues us in on his state of mind. And—owing to his prior title—the entire monologue must be written in rhyme.

Gone But Not Forgotten

How do we pay tribute to those who are no longer among the living? In a recent trip to Paris, we spent an afternoon touring Montparnasse Cemetery. Montparnasse—the final resting place of over 40,000 dearly ☐ eparted—is one of four 19ᵗʰ century Parisian burial grounds and the city's second largest after Père Lachaise. An extensive canopy of leafy shade trees tower over the wide, well-manicured avenues which are the demarcation lines of who is buried where. It's the wealth of funerary art and poignant adornments around every turn, though, which takes one's breath away, especially those symbolizing the senseless loss of soldiers' lives during World War I.

Your assignment: Compose your own fictional biography of the officer whose life is honored in this haunting image. What was his name? Who were his parents? Where did they live? Did he have a sweetheart he planned to come home to? And what defined his personal calling to go to war?

Now Arriving at the Gate

In the 1930s, artist Allen Tupper True was commissioned by Brown Palace in Denver to paint several large murals. This one, entitled *Airplane Travel*, was installed in the hotel's lobby in 1937. The idea of people being able to get from one point to another without taking a car, train or boat was heady stuff indeed during this time. In fact, many passengers viewed this form of travel as an opportunity to dress in their stylish best, a trend that has woefully fallen by the wayside in the last 80 years.

Your assignment: Who is this attractive woman deplaning with an armful of fresh flowers in her arm? Is she coming home from somewhere else or is she on vacation? Is she traveling alone or will someone else shortly emerge behind her? If so, who is it? Are the people assembled at the foot of the stairs there to greet this lady's arrival or simply waiting to board for the next flight? And what's with the man toting the golf clubs? Write a flash fiction story of 300 words or less that explores these questions.

Wish You Were Here

My paternal grandmother adored postcards. She also loved going on cruises to interesting destinations. She combined these two passions by purchasing a stack of postcards at the first port of call and then spending most of the cruise in her stateroom writing chatty notes to all of her friends about the wonderful time she was having.

In the early 19th century years of postcard-sending, the address was the *only* content allowed on the back. If the front of the card didn't contain an image, a message could be written there. Accommodation was later made for a very tiny note to be written on the side with the picture. It wasn't only 1907 that the "divided back" was developed that allowed a short message on the left and the address on the right.

Still, that doesn't leave a whole lot of room unless one's penmanship is very small or s/he knows how to embrace brevity of thought.

Your assignment: You are F. Scott Fitzgerald and your publisher wants to see the synopsis of the new project you're working on, a novel called *The Great Gatsby*. Alas, but the only thing you have to write it on and pop it into the mail right away is a postcard with a divided back.

Piece of cake, right? Sure it is. We have total confidence in you.

CHAPTER 7
HERE THERE BE MONSTERS

Like a lot of kids, I grew up thinking that monsters lived in my bedroom closet. I had no particular reason for believing this, of course, nor did I ever ponder why they could be kept so easily at bay by a Tinkerbelle nightlight, an open bedroom door and a cadre of vigilant stuffed animals. Perhaps, though, I now credit such childhood angst for the adult rationale of keeping my walk-in closet stuffed with enough apparel that any monster dumb enough to get trapped inside would likely suffocate before s/he could inflict much harm.

The writer's block exercises in this chapter all revolve around scary beasts whether they hail from other planets, mysterious laboratories, the mists of time ... or just live inside our own heads.

But first:

- What's your favorite monster movie of all time? Where did the monster come from? What were its most frightening attributes? How was it vanquished ... or was it?
- Which is scarier to you—an animal monster with human intelligence or a human monster that acts like an animal?
- What type of monster would you least like to encounter?
- What type of monster do you think would make a good friend?
- Do you believe monsters really exist?
- Think of the most frightening monster you have ever seen in a movie. What were the monster's motivations for his or her actions? Was it Reward? Revenge? Escape? If you were to rewrite this film, what changes would you make in order for the monster to be a sympathetic character that audiences would root for?

Spare Parts

During the summer of 1816, a young woman named Mary Shelley was staying at Lake Geneva in Switzerland with her future husband. A vision came to her one moonlit evening and she furiously began to compose the supernatural story of scientist Victor Frankenstein's quest to create artificial life.

Unfortunately, Victor's expectations of fashioning something beautiful that could keep him company backfired, causing him to reject his "child" in horror. Thus, exists the conundrum of having to accept the bad along with the good if you dare to go dabbling in the dark realms of reanimation.

Your Assignment: The protagonist of your story is a kindly mortician who believes that some of the dearly □ eparted in his village still have something vital to contribute.

Mr. Mullins, for instance, was an exceptional gardener.

Mrs. Mitchell never met a stray cat that she didn't welcome into her home with love.

Miss Revere, the librarian, baked the very best pies.

Mr. Turner had the strength to bend steel with his bare hands.

Mrs. Simpson was a whirling dervish when it came to her knitting needles and had gifted many a neighbor with sweaters and scarves.

Each of these individuals, however, also harbored dangerous traits the mortician wasn't aware of until he stitched them into one personality and gave it life on a dark and stormy night.

Write a one-page description of the result, give the monster a name, and tell us what the monster does on its first day loose in the village.

Hideous Hybrids

In the 1958 film, *The Fly*, a scientist playing around with matter transference accidentally swaps his head and one arm with that of a fly. (The film was remade in 1986 starring Jeff Goldblum.) In light of current controversies about modern stem cell research, the notion of fusing or splicing the DNA of unrelated species isn't all that far-fetched.

Your assignment: Choose any subject from Column A and any subject from Column B to create a hybrid monster. Give it a catchy name, define its attributes, powers and vulnerabilities, and write a one-page synopsis for a novel in which this mutant creature is the central figure.

COLUMN A	COLUMN B
Mosquito	Hippo
Boa constrictor	Triceratops
Bunny	Piranha
Alligator	Buffalo
Banana slug	Hyena
Giant Panda	Anteater
Bat	Badger
Salamander	Scorpion
Struthiomimus	Amoeba
Piglet	Stingray
Man	Woman
Spider	Wolverine
Shark	Komodo Dragon
Leech	Hornet
Canary	Tse Tse fly
King cobra	Wild boar
Madagascar fossa	Jellyfish

Jane Eyre's Twilight

Mr. Rochester, the brooding lord of Thornfield Manor, is concerned that his new governess, Jane, is spending way too much time wistfully watching the comings and goings of their new neighbors, the Cullens. In particular, she seems fixated—to the point of downright pining—on the ghostly pale and mysterious Edward.

Is it jealousy that compels Rochester to dissuade Jane from her infatuation or has he learned that Edward has a deadly secret?

Your assignment: Write a two-page scene in which Rochester shares his suspicions and forbids Jane to go on an upcoming moonlight picnic with her new beau.

Captain Ahab, Alien Chaser

Captain Ahab is a man obsessed, a man obsessed with the belief that giant leviathans from another world are roaming the planet's waters with a cunning plan to one day come ashore and vanquish all of humanity. The only way to stop them, he decides, is to hunt down their leader before it's too late. He heads to the nearest seaport tavern to recruit a fearless crew.

Your assignment: Write a one-page rousing monologue in which Ahab tries to convince his listeners that time is of the essence in mounting an attack against the giant alien invaders.

The Mummy's Great Expectations

A lot can happen when you've been under wraps for 3,000 years. Just ask Miss Havisham. Owing to a dreadful mistake, she was accidentally mummified, stuck in an Egyptian crypt, and missed her own wedding day. Fast forward to the present and her sarcophagus has been shipped to England where it's going to reside in the private collection of a young man named Pip. During a violent thunderstorm, Miss Havisham's mummy suddenly sits upright in Pip's library where he has been trolling the Internet for directions to a new dance club he has heard about.

Your assignment: Write a two-page scene in which Miss Havisham demands to know where she is and what's going on.

Home Alone

I felt I was long past the age of having a babysitter and it seemed silly that I had to be sent on a sleepover at a friend's house if my parents were going out for the evening. I finally convinced them I was old enough to stay home by myself. After all, didn't I have Nero (our Belgian Shepherd) to protect me? My ulterior motive was also to turn on a popular television show my parents strictly forbade me to watch because they thought it was a corrupting influence. Since neither one of them was inclined to look at *TV Guide*, I was confident they'd never know they were going out on the same night *The Mod Squad* was on.

After reminding me multiple times to not go outside, to make sure all of the windows were closed, and to check and double-check that all of the doors were locked, they took off for a party. They even told me that Nero could sleep in my bedroom. Honestly, were they *trying* to make me paranoid?

I had my dinner, watched television and finally decided to get ready for bed. Wait a minute! What was that noise just now? And why is it that you suddenly hear all manner of creaks and squeaks and thuds and scrapes when you're by yourself that you absolutely *never* hear when other people are around? Had Nero heard those noises, too? I called him but he was strangely fixated on the door to the hall closet, his head down and a low growl emanating from his throat.

Visions of monsters danced into my head. Was it possible that someone—or *something*—had slipped inside before my parents ever left and had been biding its time to jump out and devour me? Or is it that dogs—and quite a few cats—get bored and just like to mess with us? Oddly enough, I summoned the courage to yank the closet door open and scare *it* first with a mighty yell.

For many months after, I'm sure there were several coats and a vacuum cleaner which still trembled at the memory of that experience.

Your assignment: Make a list of 10 unusual places you would not want to be locked in by yourself on a dark and stormy night. For each venue, identify what kind of supernatural creature would be hanging out there (i.e., a zombie at a laundromat).

Skin-Deep Beauty

A chapter about monsters would be remiss if it didn't include mention of the monsters that reside within the human psyche. Just as heroes are not 100 percent good, villains are not 100 percent evil. The fine line which divides the two can be as much a product of birth as it can be a twist of fate which subsequently brings out an individual's most stellar qualities (i.e., rescuing passengers when the ship collides with an iceberg) or their darkest shortcomings (i.e., pushing the nearest women and children out of the lifeboat in order to secure a place for oneself).

In 1886, Robert Louis Stevenson explored the dualities of human nature in his gothic thriller, *The Strange Case of Dr. Jekyll and Mr. Hyde.* While the doctor was a fairly decent chap who needed funding for experiments which he felt would benefit mankind, his smelly and unkempt altar ego was a animalistic thug and murderer that ran amok whenever the potent elixir was quaffed.

In the absence of a conscience or moral center, Hyde does whatever he wants or, rather, what Jekyll is precluded from ever doing as *himself* because such vile behavior would be unseemly for someone in his social class. Nor, we suspect, would his winsome fiancée and future in-laws approve.

How could the story be different if set in the 21st century … and with a female having a split personality? Let's find out.

Your assignment: The "good" half of her persona is a plain but extremely smart woman who works in the lab of a cosmetics corporation. One day she happens upon a formula than can temporarily transform her into a real-life version of Jessica Rabbit. She's initially excited by how this changes an off-hours existence that used to be pretty dull and boring.

The downside?

The bad girl is bad with a capital B and plans to use her looks for organizing an evil cartel and taking over the world. Write a one-page synopsis of how this plot would go.

Defrosted

Hollywood has a fondness for bringing monsters out of the deep-freeze and unleashing them on modern society:

The Beast From 20,000 Fathoms
Alien vs. Predator
Mammoth
Transformers
Dinosaurus
The Thing
Monsters vs. Aliens

Sometimes, though, having monsters on ice doesn't even involve the North or South Pole or the Himalayas. In *Demolition Man* (1993) the psychopathic Simon Phoenix (Wesley Snipes) uses the opportunity of a short-term thaw for his parole hearing at the California Cryo-Penitentiary to make his escape.

Cognizant of the horrors Phoenix is capable of unleashing on the now-pacifist world of 2032, the administrators have no choice but to defrost LAPD Sergeant John Spartan (Sylvester Stallone) and send him in hot pursuit.

Your assignment: What is the scariest monster you can imagine? What if s/he was cryogenically contained for 150 years and then accidentally released into a society that, frankly, has no frame of reference for being scared by monsters because they do not believe monsters exist.

Write a flash fiction story of 300 words or less from the monster's frustrated point of view.

CHRISTINA HAMLETT

CHAPTER 8
LAWYERING UP

Why do things always get more complicated when attorneys enter the equation? This is not, by any means, a knock on the profession, especially since I'm married to someone who practices it.

It's just that certain issues, disputes and misunderstandings which could otherwise be resolved by cool heads and clear communications can get drawn out interminably when both sides decide to hire counsel to defend them. We are also, alas, living in a litigious era in which even the slightest slight becomes cause to take an adversary to the cleaners and profit from real or imagined wrongdoing.

Creating, interpreting and enforcing laws dates back to the early Egyptians. This means that squillions of cases have been tried that—unless they ended up changing history—are cases we've never even heard of. This also means it's rich fodder for making up our own attorney-centric scenarios … and that's what this chapter is all about.

The idea came to me a few years ago when I was reading a book about the lives of Henry VIII's six spouses. Henry, of course, was adept at making up rules as he went along. When the Catholic church wouldn't allow him to divorce his first wife, he turned around and started his *own* church. When his first wife died and—following the order to behead Anne Boleyn—Henry declared he was technically a widower because of his first marriage and that he could now go back to being Catholic. What a lawyer's nightmare he would have been! Yet, interestingly, Wife #1 and Wife #4 faired quite well as divorcees. Hmmm … it was almost as if a lawyer *was* involved in orchestrating their generous settlements from the king.

That premise is explored in my full-length play, *A Bel Air Lawyer in King Henry's Court*, which had its world premiere in the U.K. the summer of 2017. Henry's verbal sparring with a sharp-talking Jewish divorce attorney from the 23rd century had audiences alternatively rooting for Henry and then Jerome, each man making a solid case as to why the law should be on his side.

The script, by the by, is available for download at www.stageplays.com.

Before I Thee Wed

Yes, the glass slipper fit perfectly when Prince Charming went searching for the beautiful young woman with whom he had danced at his parentals' castle the week before. Cinderella, he announced, was the one he would live happily ever after with and raise a lovely family of little princesses and princes.

He couldn't help but notice, though, that she lived in a somewhat dodgy part of the village. A cottage with a thatched roof? Seriously? And those tattered clothes? What happened to the sparkly ball gown and that sleek, pumpkin-shaped carriage with the prancing horses?

She sweetly—and honestly—explains that these were just loaners from her fairy godmother. "But as soon as we're married, my love, and I come to live with you at your fabulous castle ...?"

"Uh, I need a moment," he replies, his mind racing feverishly. Yes, he adored her without question but seeing as how she had only her beauty and a couple greedy relatives to bring to the relationship, this was beginning to feel a bit one-sided.

Your assignment: Write a three-page scene in which Cinderella, Prince Charming and the latter's attorney sit down to discuss the particulars of a royal pre-nup agreement.

A Shoddy Environment

We never hear anything about him but the old woman who lived in the shoe did indeed have a husband. Now guilt-ridden for having deserted them all those years ago, he comes for a visit and is aghast to discover what, exactly, the kids are living in. This, he decides, is completely unacceptable. He's going to go to Child Protective Services and have the kids removed immediately. She, however, has saved up money in a sock to go hire an attorney to argue her side of the issue.

Your assignment: Write a one-page stirring monologue in which the lawyer delineates all the reasons that living in a lace-up boot with a sturdy heel is perfectly healthy.

When Z's Add Up

Librarians can get pretty zealous when it comes to overdue books, even if a person has a well-publicized excuse for the delay. When she checked out a title by her favorite YA author that fateful day, Princess Aurora had no idea that a wicked encounter with a spinning wheel would derail her otherwise punctual habit of always returning borrowed books.

After a hundred years of involuntary beauty sleep, the last thing she wanted to wake up to was a whopping bill in late fees as well as a subpoena to appear in court and explain herself.

Your assignment: Write a one-page dialogue scene between Sleeping Beauty's lawyer and the librarian. Neither side wants to back down. Oh, and their conversation also has to be written in rhyme.

Identity Theft

Remember how hard it was to get your first credit card, especially if no one had previously extended you any credit? Now imagine how much harder this would be if you refused to give the credit card company your actual name.

Rumpelstiltskin has good reason for wanting to keep his identity a secret. If a certain young miss for whom he has been spinning straw into gold should find out what he's called, the deal he has made with her will automatically be null and void.

Desperate to establish a line of credit, he consults an attorney. The crafty attorney discovers an interesting legal loophole and advises him to simply use a pseudonym. There's just a little catch.

Your assignment: The pseudonym (which can be a single name or a first/last combination) can *only* be comprised of the letters that currently exist in his true name (i.e., Rik Smelt, Mel Punstir, R.K. Pest). Challenge yourself to come up with as many names as you can.

What's Mine Is Mine
(Unless It Was Previously Yours)

It has always been said that one man's trash is another man's treasure. In the case of this writing assignment, sometimes it can even be property that was stolen during a burglary.

The set-up is a neighborhood garage sale. The homeowners—caught up in the zeal of Spring housecleaning—have laid out a diverse spread of merchandise. Everything is going well until one of the shoppers happens to notice that a number of items for sale are his/her own property which had gone missing the previous year. Are the homeowners secretly cat burglars? Did they receive these items from someone they trusted? Is the shopper simply wanting to make an ugly scene in order to get a lower price and score a better sale? Or could it be that the merchandise was originally stolen by the shopper and then subsequently stolen by the neighbor? Can a call to an attorney to resolve all of this be far behind?

Your assignment: Write a one-page synopsis for a novel that gets to the bottom of this suburban mystery.

A Bard By Any Other Name

Conspiracy theories abound as to who might have written all of the works attributed to William Shakespeare. Among the most popular candidates are his contemporaries Ben Jonson, Edward de Ver, and Christopher Marlowe. But what if the real author was someone whose day job precluded much dabbling in fluffy theatricals? What if Shakespeare himself—a public servant invention—was nothing more than a clever cover to gauge public opinion about the monarchy?

Your assignment: Yes, you read it here first. Queen Elizabeth was an aspiring playwright who couldn't easily produce material under her own name. Write a three-page scene in which her lawyer tries to convince her that she should go public with her moonlighting activities.

Pretty Liar

In Greek mythology, the daughter of Queen Hecuba and King Priam was given the gift of prophecy. While such a talent could certainly come in handy for helping others meet their true soul mates, make discoveries of treasure or determine the outcome of wars before the first battle cry was ever issued, there was one pesky little obstacle that Cassandra couldn't overcome: none of her predictions would be believed by her listeners.

Your assignment: A modern-day Cassandra is a Manhattan lawyer who needs to convince the law firm where she works to follow her advice on an important business matter or else risk losing the entire company. Since she knows the truth won't be believed no matter how earnestly she imparts it, she realizes the only way to achieve her objective is to keep saying the opposite. Write a two-page scene in which she puts this artful strategy to the test.

Bearly Plausible

It's hard to argue that the three bears didn't have an awfully good case against Goldilocks. She broke into their house, she ate their baby's breakfast, she destroyed a perfectly good chair and then she had the nerve to bounce around on their beds before finally falling asleep. Yep, this is pretty much open and shut and the bears are ready to hire a good lawyer and sue for damages.

Except ...

Your assignment: Goldilocks hires her own attorney to fight the bears' claims of wrongdoing. Write her attorney's one-page opening statement which will seek to prove that his/her client burnt her tongue on porridge that was too hot, sustained injuries from a poorly constructed homemade chair, and was overcome by mold issues in the bedding that caused her to lose consciousness.

CHAPTER 9
SCHENECTADY IDEA SERVICE

Back in the days I ran a touring theatre company, we used to debut 12-16 original one-act plays per year. Since our audiences knew that these were all penned by yours truly, it wasn't uncommon for me to be asked, "So where do you get your ideas?" The honest answer—that the plots were inspired by real life, by classic literature, and by historical events—never seemed to satisfy anyone. Writers, they seemed to assume, had access to secret vaults, possessed mystical powers, or received ongoing satellite transmissions from Saturn.

One evening when I was asked this question by an aspiring author, I whimsically responded that I had a subscription to The Schenectady Idea Service and was supplied new plots for $5.00 a month. He thought about this a moment before replying, "Yeah, I figured it had to be something like that since no one could possibly come up with so much stuff on their own."

Hmm.

Although to my knowledge no such service exists, this chapter offers the next best thing: A list of 50 free story-starters to turn into wildly creative projects. As you pick and choose which ones you like, consider the following elements:

- ✓ What genre is the best fit for this story-starter?
- ✓ What time period will comfortably accommodate the plot and characters?
- ✓ What is the physical setting for the action?
- ✓ Who is the hero? Who is the villain?
- ✓ What is at stake that will compel your character(s) to take risks?
- ✓ How will the story be resolved in a satisfying manner for your readers?

The Story Starters

1. A genie grants your main character a super-power … but only for a single day.
2. A chemistry student makes a huge discovery that his/her teacher wants to steal.
3. Two competitive DJ's try to boost their ratings through outlandish stunts.
4. A Halloween prank goes horribly wrong.
5. A cryogenically frozen body is defrosted a century later.
6. The new owner of a company fires everyone on the first day.
7. A wealthy couple—now suddenly broke—enter the work force as domestics.
8. A lonely character comes home from work to discover an abandoned child sitting on his/her doorstep with a cryptic note pinned on its sweater.
9. A teen with no work experience inherits a run-down ski lodge.
10. A musical prodigy finds herself/himself competing against a serious crush.
11. A housesitting job in a foreign country turns into something much more serious.
12. Three astronauts learn that their upcoming "flight" to Mars is going to actually be televised from a Hollywood sound stage.
13. A journalist pens a fake news story that subsequently wins a major award.
14. An eccentric millionaire leaves his/her entire estate to his/her Pomeranian.
15. A housewife auditions for a local variety show.
16. A woman lets a cute guy borrow her car at a party to make a liquor run; instead he uses it to rob a convenience store.
17. A new manager discovers that his entire staff is comprised of snarky robots.

18. A parent notices that his/her toddler becomes furry and grows claws and fangs every time the moon is full.
19. A pair of ice skaters assume they'll be going to the Winter Olympics as a team … until s/he is teamed up with someone else.
20. A thunderstorm and mudslide causes a strange diary to show up on someone's doorstep.
21. A pair of long-distance pen pals exaggerate about their personal lives.
22. An employee learns through an overheard conversation that s/he is about to be terminated.
23. At a high school reunion, a woman discovers her former hunky crush is living out of his car.
24. A protagonist who uses a ghostwriter for his/her books is asked to host a cooking show.
25. A well-intentioned parent mistakenly invites his/her teen's worst enemy on a vacation.
26. A tax preparer makes a massive mistake on a client's filing.
27. A psychic makes the shocking discovery she no longer has any precognition powers.
28. Two celebrities show up on the red carpet wearing exactly the same outfit.
29. A marriage counselor falls in love with the husband of one of her clients.
30. Your protagonist discovers an unattended laptop displaying the code to a treasure map.
31. "Bring your child to work day" has unexpected consequences.
32. An author receives his/her first rejection letter.
33. A teen comes home well past curfew and discovers the entire house is spookily empty.
34. A dream house turns out to be a nightmare.
35. A CEO decides to bypass his/her oldest son/daughter and name a total stranger as successor to the company.

36. A previously missed inscription in an old yearbook changes everything.
37. A department store window dresser becomes obsessed with someone s/he observes every evening in the apartment building across the street.
38. An octogenarian decides to celebrate his/her birthday by bungee jumping off a bridge.
39. A magician's trick at a birthday party turns all the kids into mice.
40. The members of a garage band can't decide on the "perfect" name for their label.
41. The excavation to build a multi-story condo development reveals an ancient burial ground.
42. A successful businessperson lives in fear of his/her secret being revealed.
43. Genealogy research reveals an unsettling gap in facts long held to be true.
44. A teenager finds out that her father is going to marry the mom of her worst enemy at school.
45. A volunteer selling tickets door-to-door witnesses a murder.
46. For an environmental cause she believes in, a woman decides to hike cross-country with nothing more than a backpack.
47. A safe deposit box yields an unexpected link to an unsolved crime.
48. A character takes a selfie and is startled to see what is revealed in the background.
49. A character discovers s/he can precisely script what dreams will come every night.
50. An adoptee decides to find his/her birth parents despite warnings this quest will not have a happy ending.

One Size Fits Everyone

Okay, I know exactly what you're thinking:

"Unless I am the only person who bought this book and just read the 50 freebie story-starters, there are a squillion *other* writers out there who might pick the very same plot that *I* want to write."

Yes, there's always that possibility. There are also two things for you to keep in mind:

1. As the author of this book, I *want* there to be a squillion writers who buy it and read it cover to cover.
2. Stories are events which are filtered through the mind of every individual. Accordingly, it's each individual's personal experience and frame of reference which will determine *how* any given story is expressed.

The story-starters on the previous pages have all been used in live workshops, the participants being instructed to each choose an idea that appeals to them and decide how to develop it for stage, page or cinema. Yet no matter the size of the group or the number of times a particular story-starter is chosen, the plots which emerge have unanimously gone in totally different directions.

Let's see how this works with a couple random picks.

An adoptee decides to find his/her birth parents despite warnings this quest will not have a happy ending.
The circa could be Colonial America, 19th century France, modern-day China or even outer space. The gender of the adoptee could influence the resources and social support to initiate the search. *Why* does the adoptee want to reconnect? Is s/he seeking a familial match for medical reasons? To chase down an inheritance? To get closure following years of confusion associated with abandonment?

A teenager finds out that her father is going to marry the mom of her worst enemy at school.

The premise could be ripe for a television sitcom in which the teen conspires and schemes every week with her friends to get her dad to fall in love with someone else or to convince her nemesis that marrying into such a social lame family will cause her popularity to plummet. But what if instead of a comedy you were to turn this into a horror story? In order to thwart the impending nuptials, the desperate teen starts dabbling in the dark side and unleashes a solution more terrifying than the very problem she was trying to solve?

A character takes a selfie and is startled to see what is revealed in the background.

Could it be a ghost? A celebrity? Bigfoot? A former flame who disappeared 10 years ago? A story-starter such as this could unfold in any type of setting … but what if the image revealed in the background is what that setting looked like over a century ago? Can it be that the spot the character is standing on is an operating portal to the past?

A thunderstorm and mudslide causes a strange diary to show up on someone's doorstep.

A premise such as this would work in any circa or, for that matter, in any country. If the structure incorporates flashbacks to reveal the diary as a work-in-progress, a minimalist stage play or a film script would serve it well. The question might also be posed as to whether it was the storm which caused the diary to be dislodged from a hiding place or whether it was physically placed on the doorstep by someone who is using it as a favor … or a threat.

Finding The 25th Hour

Could your writing schedule use an extra hour? Of course it could, but to paraphrase Captain Jack Sparrow from *Pirates of the Caribbean*, "The Isla de More Time cannot be found except by those who already know where it is." If you want to keep to a code of high productivity and keep writer's block at bay, it starts with aggressive decluttering. For a single day, record exactly how much time you spend checking email, surfing the Internet, reading TMZ gossip, looking for lost notes, playing computer games. Yikes! Who'd have imagined how it all adds up!

- If you live with others, how often do they interrupt and derail your train of thought? Writing is your job. Insist on respect.
- Learn keyboard shortcuts to save typing time. (http://www.microsoft.com/enable/products/keyboard.aspx)
- Consolidate or delegate your errand-running.
- Identify your most productive writing zone and consistently stick to it.
- Remove distractions from your workspace.
- Get up earlier; go to bed later.
- Invest in electronic programs such as NewNovelist, StoryCraft, Quick Story, Writer's Café, Writer's Blocks or even voice recognition software. For aspiring screenwriters, a software program such as Final Draft not only puts all of the elements in the right place but saves valuable time trying to set industry standard margins and dialogue blocks manually in Word.
- Use rewards—a spa day, chocolate, new shoes—to stay motivated. (Didn't you always do your homework faster when you knew you could go play afterwards?)
- Set goals related to word/page output rather than "x" amount of time physically spent in front of your monitor. Some people can turn out one page in ten minutes while others struggle with that same page for an entire hour. Committing to sit at your computer for an hour everyday doesn't mean anything if the maximum you compose is half a sentence.

Need additional resources to get yourself organized? Try these:

- *168 Hours: You Have More Time Than You Think* by Laura Vanderkam
- *A Writer's Time: Making the Time to Write* by Kenneth Atchity
- *The Coffee Break Screenwriter: Writing Your Script Ten Minutes at a Time* by Pilar Alessandra
- *Time Management Master: How To Become More Efficient and Accomplish Everything You Want In Less Time You Ever Thought Possible* by Vanessa Pagan
- *10 Minute Time Management: The Stress-Free Guide to Getting Stuff Done* by Ric Thompson
- *The 7 Secrets of the Prolific: The Definitive Guide to Overcoming Procrastination, Perfectionism, and Writer's Block* by Hillary Rettig
- *Avoid Social Media Time Suck: A Blueprint for Writers to Create Online Buzz for Their Books and Still Have Time to Write* by Frances Caballo
- *Business For Authors: How To Be An Author Entrepreneur* by Joanna Penn

EPILOGUE:
BECOME THE BLOCK-BUSTER
YOU WERE MEANT TO BE

Now and again in your career as a wordsmith, writer's block will try to slither in and disrupt the creative flow. If and when this happens, here's a passel of plucky tips to get you back on track.

Move away from the keyboard and pick up a pencil. Or a crayon. When you become so accustomed to using the same tools day-in and day-out, you start blaming them for your own boredom. When you use something you've been away from for a while (including, quite possibly, since childhood), it's a fresh experience that causes you to wonder what you can do with it (including doodling).

Talk out loud to yourself. As someone who spent years in theatre, I not only do this on a regular basis but also with different accents. Use the course of this imaginary dialogue to brainstorm ideas, argue the pros and cons, and give yourself a good old fashioned pep talk. If you do the latter with a British accent, you'll be amazed how much smarter you feel. "I say there, ol' chap, what's this sticky wicket muddle all about? It's not as if we haven't been here before. And if I may be so bold, I *must* say that your handling of the last go-round was nothing short of brill!"

Impose cliffhangers as you go. Stop typing in the middle of a sentence, even if you know how that sentence is going to end. Do this right before you go to bed. Your brain will be absolutely itching to finish that sentence first thing in the morning ... and will also have been churning throughout the night with ideas on the *new* sentences which will follow. Keep in mind that if you give yourself too easy a place to stop (i.e., the end of a chapter), you're making it that much harder to restart when it's time to begin the next chapter.

Reset your writing clock. If you always struggle to write anything midday on an empty stomach, switch things up and start writing in the morning after breakfast or in the evening right after dinner.

Write in a different room. If you do most of your writing at a dining room table, sit in the opposite chair. Every time you look up, it will be to a view you typically have your back to.

Flip through family photo albums and examine them in a different way. For instance, did you and your siblings always line up in exactly the same way for holiday pictures? Does your Uncle Bob always wear the same sweater vest? How many objects can you identify in the backgrounds that you never really noticed before?

Buy a CD of nature sounds (i.e., thunderstorms, birds twittering, surf pounding the shore). Close your eyes and listen to it. Picture scenes in your head to match what you're hearing.

Purchase a word-a-day calendar. Whatever the word is, use it in 20 different sentences before you can move back to whatever it is you're currently stuck on. And, of course, the side benefit is that you're learning new words in the process.

Do a Google search for The 10 Worst Jobs or check out http://www.careercast.com/jobs-rated. This will remind you of all the drekky employment you might be forced to take if you let writer's block win and this writing gig doesn't pan out.

Dance like no one is watching. You won't just burn off calories; you will also re-energize yourself. You can likewise engage in activities such as aggressively vacuuming, scrubbing the floors, washing your car, etc. Dancing, though, is probably more fun.

Rearrange your bookshelves alphabetically or by author/genre. In the process, you'll familiarize yourself with writers whose work you admire. Fantasize that someday another aspiring author will be rearranging his/her bookshelves and thinking about *you*.

Take a distance-learning class that has nothing to do with the craft of writing.

Come up with 10 original titles a day and record them in an idea book.

Play word association games with yourself.

Listen to music that typically isn't your style.

Give yourself permission to take a break, to do something silly, to eat your favorite comfort food, to go to a movie.

Remind yourself of why you wanted to become a writer in the first place.

Take a long walk around your neighborhood.

Hug your dog. Why? Because dogs are nonjudgmental and will continue to love you and believe in you even on the days you don't necessarily believe in yourself.

ABOUT THE AUTHOR

Photo Credit: Mark Webb

Former actress and director Christina Hamlett is an award-winning author whose credits to date include 40 books, 165 stage plays, 5 optioned feature films, and squillions of articles and interviews that appear online and in trade publications worldwide. She is also a script consultant for stage and screen (which means she stops a lot of really bad plots from coming to theatres near you) and a professional ghostwriter (which does not mean she talks to dead people).

She and her gourmet chef husband and Lucy, the world's cutest dog, reside in Southern California.

To learn more, visit her website at www.authorhamlett.com.